done in a flash

D1591973

done in a flash

100 speedy wok and stove-top stir-fries

southwater

This edition is published by Southwater

Southwater is an imprint of Anness Publishing Ltd
Hermes House, 88–89 Blackfriars Road, London SE1 8HA
tel. 020 7401 2077; fax 020 7633 9499
www.southwaterbooks.com;
info@anness.com

Published in the USA by Southwater,
Anness Publishing Inc.
fax 212 807 6813

This edition distributed in the UK by
The Manning Partnership
tel. 01225 852 727; fax 01225 852 852;

This edition distributed in the USA by
National Book Network
tel. 301 459 3366; fax 301 459 1705;

This edition distributed in Canada by
General Publishing
tel. 416 445 3333; fax 416 445 5991;

This edition distributed in Australia by
Sandstone Publishing
tel. 02 9560 7888; fax 02 9560 7488;

This edition distributed in New Zealand by
The Five Mile Press (NZ) Ltd
tel. (09) 444 4144; fax (09) 444 4518

Publisher: Joanna Lorenz
Managing Editor: Linda Fraser
Designers: Adrian Morris and Peter Laws
Photographers: Amanda Heywood and Michelle Garrett
Home economists: Nicola Fowler and Liz Trigg

Previously published as *A Flash in the Pan*

1 3 5 7 9 10 8 6 4 2

NOTES
For all recipes, quantities are given in both metric and imperial measures and, where
appropriate, measures are also given in standard cups and spoons. Follow one set,
but not a mixture, because they are not interchangeable.

Standard spoon and cup measures are level.
1 tsp = 5ml, 1 tbsp = 15ml, 1 cup = 250ml/8fl oz

Australian standard tablespoons are 20ml. Australian readers should use 3 tsp in place of 1 tbsp for
measuring small quantities of gelatine, cornflour, salt, etc.
Medium eggs are used unless otherwise stated.

CONTENTS

INTRODUCTION

Stir-frying is an ancient cooking technique that originated in the Far East, but its popularity has spread throughout the world. It is an ideal technique for the modern cook: dishes can be stir-fried in a matter of minutes, using very little oil, which means the ingredients lose little of their nutritional value, and are relatively low in fat.

Many of the recipes in this book are Oriental favourites, originating from all over the Far East, but traditional Western dishes have been adapted to take advantage of this quick technique – you'll find recipes for Beef Sukiyaki and Duck and Ginger Chop Suey, Chicken Liver Stir-fry and stir-fried Turkey with Sage. Don't be afraid to try the recipes if you haven't got a wok – a large frying pan with a heavy base will work just as well, although you may find in some cases it is necessary to cook the ingredients in smaller batches.

Once you begin, you'll be amazed at the versatility of the technique, and may find you can adapt some of your own favourites. Whether you want a spicy starter or a sizzling dessert, consider stir-frying for a quick, healthy and delicious dish.

Equipment

You will find most of the cooking equipment you have around the kitchen will produce good results. As mentioned previously, it isn't even essential to use a wok. However, if you would like to invest in some good kitchen equipment, or wish to use the authentic tools of the trade, the following may be of interest:

Bamboo skewers
These are widely used for barbecues and grilled foods. They are discarded after use.

Chopping board
A good quality chopping board with a thick surface will last for years.

Chopping knife
If you are not comfortable using a cleaver, a large, heavy chopping knife can be used.

Citrus zester
This tool is designed to remove the zest while leaving the bitter white pith. It can also be used for shaving fresh coconut.

Cleaver
The weight of the cleaver makes it ideal for chopping all kinds of ingredients. Keep this as sharp as possible.

Cooking chopsticks
These are extra-long, and allow you to stir ingredients in the wok, while keeping a safe distance.

Draining wire
This is designed to sit on the side of the wok, and is used mainly for deep-frying.

Food processor
This is a quick alternative to the pestle and mortar.

Ladle
A long-handled ladle is very useful for spooning out soup, stock or sauces.

Pestle and mortar
This is useful for grinding small amounts of spices.

Rice paddle
This is used to fluff up rice after cooking.

Saucepan
A good saucepan with a tight-fitting lid is essential for cooking rice properly. It may also be used for stir-frying.

Sharpening stone
A traditional tool for sharpening knives and cleavers, available from hardware stores.

Stainless steel skimmer
This can be used when strong flavours are likely to affect bare metal cooking implements.

Wire skimmer
This is used to remove cooked food from boiling water or hot fat. It should not be used with fish-based liquids as the strong flavour is likely to affect the metal.

Wok
The shape of the wok allows ingredients to be cooked in a minimum of fat, thus retaining freshness and flavour. There are several varieties available including the carbon steel round-bottomed wok or Pau wok. This wok is best suited to a gas hob, where you will be able to control the amount of heat needed more easily. The carbon steel flat-bottomed wok is best for use on electric or solid fuel hobs, as it will give a better distribution of heat. A small round-bottomed wok enables you to prepare small quantities quickly, as it takes less time to heat up.

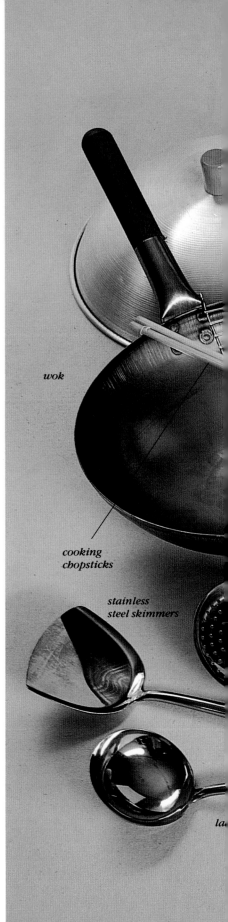

wok

cooking chopsticks

stainless steel skimmers

la...

food processor

bamboo skewers

saucepan

chopping board

chopping knife

draining wire

sharpening stone

citrus zester

cleavers

pestle and mortar

rice paddle

wire skimmer

Fresh Produce

Almost any ingredient can be stir-fried, and, as the freshness and flavour of the produce will not be affected by cooking, it is important to choose the freshest, best quality ingredients you can.

Baby sweetcorn
These may be stir-fried whole or chopped.

Beansprouts
These impart a lovely texture to vegetable and meat dishes. Do not keep for longer than a few days before using or they will brown and wilt.

Chinese lettuce
The crispy leaves are ideal for stir-frying. Shred or chop finely before using.

Coconut
Fresh coconut is infinitely better tasting than any other coconut product available. When selecting a coconut, choose one with plenty of milk inside.

Cucumber
Cucumber can be chopped and sliced finely and stir-fried, or used in relishes to accompany main dishes.

Fennel
Slice and stir-fry to impart an aniseed flavour.

Garlic
Crush or chop finely.

Leeks
Slice into very thin rings before stir-frying.

Lemons
Use the grated rind and juice in stir-fries and marinades, and lemon slices as a garnish.

Limes
Use the grated rind and juice in stir-fries and marinades, and lime slices as a garnish.

Lychees
Peel to use, remove the stone, and halve or slice.

Mango
Ripe mango should have a slightly soft flesh. Peel and remove the stone before use.

Mooli
This has a very subtle flavour.

Mustard and cress
This is usually added at the last moment, or as a garnish.

Onions
Every variety of onion makes a tasty addition to stir-fries.

Oyster mushrooms
Use as ordinary mushrooms,

wiping clean with a damp cloth or paper towel.

Patty pan squash
These small squash have a taste similar to marrow.

Peppers
Deseed and chop into strips before stir-frying.

Radishes
Slice finely, or use tiny baby radishes as a garnish.

Shitake mushrooms
These tasty, firm-textured mushrooms may be treated as ordinary mushrooms. Only use half the amount if using the dried variety. Soak in boiling water for 20 minutes, and save the soaking water for a sauce.

Spinach
Remove the stalks before using and wash thoroughly in several changes of cold water to remove any grit.

Spring onions
Chop finely before using, or cut into julienne strips.

Anti-clockwise from top left: *red peppers, coconut, lychees, shitake mushrooms, spinach, onions, beansprouts, mustard and cress, Chinese lettuce, cucumber, mooli, radish, baby sweetcorn, spring onions, leeks, oyster and shitake mushrooms, yellow pepper, fennel, celery.* In centre basket, from top left: *patty pan squash, mango, limes, garlic, lemons.*

Herbs and Spices

The following can be used to enhance fresh ingredients. Whenever possible, use fresh herbs for the best flavour. If using dried herbs you will need smaller amounts as the flavour is less subtle. Some of the flavourings used in this book include the following:

Chillies
Generally, the smallest chillies are the hottest. Removing the seeds will reduce the heat. Chop finely, and stir-fry with oil. Always work in a well-ventilated area and do not allow chillies to come into contact with your skin or eyes.

Chilli powder
Many varieties of dried chilli powder are now available, each varying in strength.

Chinese chives
These have a mild flavour similar to a Spanish onion. They should be cooked very lightly and are wonderful served raw as a garnish.

Coriander leaves
Fresh coriander imparts a unique, refreshing taste and aroma. Bunches of fresh leaves can be kept for up to 5 days in a jar of water.

Coriander seeds
Whole seeds can be dry-fried (without oil) with other ingredients and are also available ground.

Cumin
Cumin is generally dry-fried and combines well with coriander seeds. It is widely used in beef dishes.

Galingale
This is sometimes known as Lengkuas. This root has a mingled flavour of pine and citrus. It may be peeled and treated in the same way as root ginger. It is available from Oriental stores.

Lemon grass
This aromatic herb has a thin tapering stem and a citrusy, verbena flavour. To use, thinly slice the bulb end of the root.

Lime leaves
These are often called kaffir lime leaves. They are excellent in marinades, and often need to be bruised to release the flavour.

Paprika
Paprika is made from a variety of sweet red pepper. It is mild in flavour, and adds colour. Add to stir-fries or sprinkle on finished dishes.

Parsley
Parsley, both curly and flat-leaf, is an ideal and attractive garnish. Flat-leaf parsley has a stronger flavour than the curly variety.

Root ginger
Peel off the skin of the fresh root and use sliced, chopped or grated. Always buy the root with the smoothest skin as it is the freshest. The flesh should be a creamy colour, and not too yellow.

Rosemary
This is usually added to lamb and pork dishes. It has a strong flavour.

Star anise
This spice has a pungent, aniseed-like taste. It can either be ground, or used whole in marinades.

Turmeric
Turmeric is used for its attractive yellow colouring. It has a slightly musty taste and aroma.

Right: *Flavour enhancers for stir-fries might include herbs such as parsley, rosemary, or coriander, or spices such as chilli powder, cumin, paprika, turmeric, ginger or star anise. Lemon grass, lime leaves, galingale or fresh chillies will add a distinctly eastern flavour.*

Flavouring Ingredients

The following ingredients can be used to create authentic tasting Eastern stir-fries. They can be purchased in most large supermarkets or Oriental food stores.

Creamed coconut
This is available in a solid block form from Oriental food stores and large supermarkets and is ideal for giving an intense coconut flavour. Simply add water to make a thick coconut paste. The paste may be thinned with more water until the correct consistency and flavour is acquired.

Extra-virgin olive oil
This is the highest grade olive oil and has a very intense flavour. Do not use this oil for cooking, but drizzle it over the finished dish before serving.

Grapeseed oil
A lightly flavoured oil, good for stir-frying delicately flavoured foods.

Hoisin sauce
This is often called barbecue sauce, and is a spicy/smoky condiment with a distinctive smoky flavour.

Olive oil
The characteristic flavour of olive oil is not suitable for Oriental stir-fries. Use when you want to impart a Mediterranean flavour.

Oyster sauce
Made from oyster extract, this speciality sauce is used in many fish dishes, soups and sauces.

Peanut butter
This can be used in Indonesian satay dishes. It makes a good sauce when heated. Use varieties without sugar for the best flavour.

Red chilli sauce
A sweet, hot sauce that is often used to flavour home-made sauces, or used on its own as a dip.

Red wine vinegar
Use this vinegar for sauces, dressings and marinades for a robust flavour.

Sake (rice wine)
Sake is used mainly in Japanese stir-fries. The best grades are used for drinking, and the lower grades for sauces and marinades, and also for dressings.

Sesame oil
This is used more as a flavouring than for cooking. It is very intensely flavoured, so only a few drops will be needed at a time.

Sherry vinegar
Use for sauces and marinades for a strong flavour.

Soy sauce
Dark soy sauce is sweet and thick, and the best variety is made from naturally fermented soy. Light soy sauce is a less intense version of the classic dark soy sauce.

Sugar
Both white caster sugar and soft brown sugar are used in marinades and sauces.

Sunflower oil
A good all-purpose cooking oil with a mild flavour.

Teriyaki sauce
Use in barbecued and stir-fried dishes, and as a marinade for meat or fish.

White wine vinegar
Use for sauces, marinades and dressings.

sesame oil

olive oil

creamed coconut

red sau

brown sugar

white wine vinegar

sake (rice wine)

extra-virgin olive oil

sherry vinegar

sunflower oil

grapeseed oil

red wine vinegar

peanut butter

light soy sauce

oyster sauce

dark soy sauce

teriyaki sauce

boisin sauce

sugar

Vegetables and Storecupboard Ingredients

Most of the vegetables used in this book will be familiar to you, but descriptions of some of the more exotic ones are given below for those who are more adventurous. Remember always to buy the best and freshest vegetables and cook them for only a short time so that they retain their crispness, colour and nutrients.

Baby Sweetcorn
Little young corn cobs have a crunchy texture and a mild, sweet flavour. Buy cobs with a bright yellow colour with no brown markings. They are widely available from supermarkets and oriental grocers.

Bamboo Shoots
These mild-flavoured tender shoots of the young bamboo are widely available fresh or sliced and halved in cans. Clean thoroughly before use.

Beansprouts
These shoots of the mung bean are usually available from supermarkets. They add a crisp texture to stir-fries.

Chinese Cabbage
Also known as Chinese leaves. It looks like a large, tightly packed cos lettuce with firm, pale green, crinkled leaves. It has a delicious crunchy texture.

Chinese Pancakes
These are flour-and-water pancakes with no seasonings or spices added. They are available fresh or frozen; if using frozen pancakes, thaw them thoroughly before steaming them.

Gram Flour
Gram flour is made from ground chick-peas and has a unique flavour. It is well worth seeking out in Indian food stores or healthfood shops, but you can use plain wholemeal flour instead, adding extra water.

Mange-touts
These tender green peapods containing flat, barely formed peas are highly valued for their crisp texture and sweet subtle flavour.

Mushrooms
Both fresh and dried mushrooms can be used in wok cookery to add texture and flavour to a dish. Dried mushrooms need to be soaked in warm water for 20–30 minutes before use. The soaking liquor can be used as a stock. Although dried mushrooms are expensive per pack, only a few are needed per recipe and they store indefinitely.

Noodles
An almost bewildering variety of fresh and dried noodles is available which can be interchanged in most recipes. Some need quick cooking; others need soaking in boiling water. They can be made from wheat, rice, ground beans or buckwheat. Follow the cooking instructions on the packet.

Pak Choi
An attractive vegetable with a long, smooth, milky-white stem and large, dark green leaves.

Rice
For the purposes of this book long grain white rice is used, varying from Thai jasmine to Indian basmati. Long grain rices such as patna and basmati tend to be drier and with the grains separate when cooked; Thai jasmine rice, although delicious, is soft, light and slightly stickier. Directions for cooking rice will be found in individual recipes.

Shallots
Shallots are small mild-flavoured members of the onion family with copper-red skins. They can be used in the same way as onions or ground into Thai curry pastes or fried into crisp flakes to be used as a garnish.

Spring Onions
The long slender spring onion is the immature bulb of the yellow onion. When recipes in this book refer to the "white" part it is to the firm, essentially white section which makes up most of the onion; "green" is the leaves.

Spring Roll Wrappers
Paper-thin wrappers made from wheat flour or rice flour and water. They are available in various sizes from most oriental grocers. Wheat flour wrappers are sold frozen and need to be thawed and carefully separated before use. Rice wrappers are dry and must be gently soaked before use.

Tofu
Tofu is also known as bean curd. Blocks of firm tofu are used in the recipes in this book as it is more suitable for stir-frying and deep frying. Although rather bland in flavour, it readily absorbs the flavours of the foods with which it is cooked. Tofu can be stored in the fridge for several days covered with water.

Water Chestnuts
A walnut-sized bulb of an Asian water plant that resembles a chestnut with its outer brown layer. Once peeled, the flesh is crisp and sweet. They are sold fresh by some oriental grocers, but are more readily available canned, whole or sliced.

Wonton Wrappers
Paper-thin squares of yellow-coloured dough, these are sold in most oriental food stores.

Yard-long Beans
These are long thin beans similar to French beans but three or four times longer. Cut into smaller lengths and use just like ordinary green beans.

Top shelf, left to right: *egg noodles, wonton wrappers, water chestnuts, cellophane noodles, gram flour, spring roll wrappers*

Middle shelf, left to right: *dried Chinese mushrooms, pak choi, tofu, egg noodles, Chinese pancakes*

Bottom, left to right: *rice, (in basket) mange-touts, baby sweetcorn, shallots, shiitake mushrooms, bamboo shoots, beansprouts, Chinese cabbage, spring onions, yard-long beans*

At front: *wood ears (mushrooms)*

Preparing Ingredients

While stir-frying is quick and easy, it is essential to know how to prepare ingredients for cooking in order to be successful. Oriental cooks always use a cleaver for these tasks, but a sharp heavy knife can be used instead. For the ingredients to cook as quickly as possible and absorb the taste of the oil and flavourings despite the short cooking time, they should be cut into small uniform pieces and as many cut surfaces as possible should be exposed to the heat. Another reason for careful cutting is to enhance the visual appeal of a dish. This is why most oriental cuisines are so specific about cutting techniques, particularly vegetables.

COOK'S TIP
Because ingredients are cooked for the minimum amount of time in a wok, use only the freshest of vegetables and only premium cuts of meat and poultry bought the same day.

VEGETABLES

Some vegetables such as broccoli and cauliflower are cut according to their natural shape into florets; others are sliced, diagonally sliced, shredded, diced or roll cut depending on the dish.

1 Diagonal cutting is a technique used for cutting vegetables such as carrots, asparagus or spring onions. It allows more of the surface of the vegetable to be exposed for quicker cooking. Simply angle the cleaver or knife at a slant and cut.

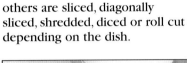
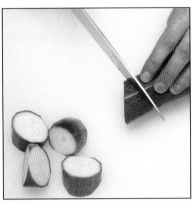

2 Roll cutting is like diagonal cutting but is used for larger vegetables such as courgettes, aubergines or large carrots. Start by making one diagonal slice at one end of the vegetable, then turn it 180° and make the next diagonal cut. Continue until you have cut the entire vegetable into even-size chunks.

MEAT

Meat for stir-frying and sometimes steaming is cut into thin slices, matchstick strips or cubes. This way it can be quickly stir-fried or steamed without losing any of its tenderness.

1 Beef is always cut across the grain otherwise it would become tough; pork, lamb and chicken can be cut either along or across the grain.

2 Placing the meat in the freezer for about 1 hour beforehand makes it easier to cut paper-thin slices.

CHOPPING HERBS

1 Strip the leaves from the stalks and pile them on a chopping board.

2 Using a cleaver or chef's knife, cut the herbs into small pieces, moving the blade back and forth until the herbs are as coarse or fine as you wish.

PEELING AND CHOPPING LEMON GRASS

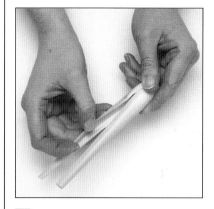

1 Cut off and discard the dry leafy tops, leaving about 15 cm/6 in of stalk. Peel away any tough outer layers from the lemon grass.

2 Lay the lemon grass on a board. Set a cleaver or chef's knife on top and strike it firmly with your fist – this helps to extract maximum flavour. Cut across the lemon grass to make thin slices, then continue chopping until fine.

PREPARING BEANSPROUTS

1 Pick over the beansprouts, discarding any that are discoloured, broken or wilted.

2 Rinse the beansprouts under cold running water and drain well.

PREPARING KAFFIR LIME LEAVES

1 Using a small sharp knife, remove the centre vein.

2 Cut the leaves crossways into very fine strips.

PEELING AND CHOPPING GARLIC

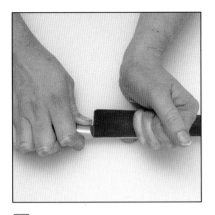 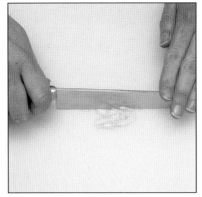

1 Lay the unpeeled garlic clove on a board. Set the flat side of a cleaver or chef's knife on top and strike it firmly with your fist.

2 Peel off and discard the skin. Finely chop the garlic, using the cleaver, moving the blade back and forth.

CUTTING AND SHREDDING GARLIC AND GINGER

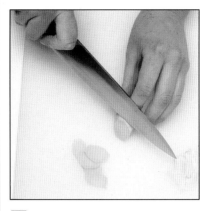 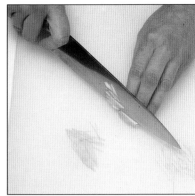

1 Peel the skin from the root ginger or garlic clove. Using a cleaver or chef's knife, cut into thin slices.

2 To cut into shreds, arrange the slices one on top of another and cut lengthways into fine strips.

PEELING AND CHOPPING GINGER

 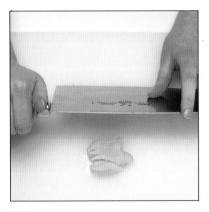 

1 Using a small sharp knife, peel the skin from the root ginger.

2 Place the ginger on a board. Set the flat side of a cleaver or chef's knife on top and strike it firmly with your fist – this will soften its fibrous texture.

3 Chop the ginger as coarsely or finely as you wish, moving the blade backwards and forwards.

REMOVING SEEDS FROM CHILLIES

1 Wearing rubber gloves, remove the stalks from chillies.

2 Cut in half lengthways.

3 Using a small sharp knife, scrape out the seeds and fleshy white ribs from each half.

Garnishes

Many Asian dishes rely on garnishes to add a colourful finishing decorative touch. The garnishes can be simple, such as chopped coriander, fresh herb sprigs, or finely shredded spring onions or chilli, or more elaborate, such as cucumber fans, spring onion brushes and chilli flowers.

CHILLI FLOWER

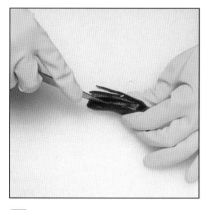

1 Make several lengthways cuts through a chilli from below the stalk to the tip. Remove and discard any seeds.

2 Soak the chilli in iced water until the ends curl to form a "flower". Pat dry with kitchen paper before use.

CUCUMBER FAN

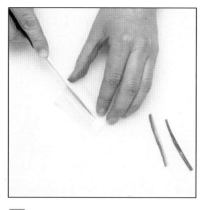

1 Cut a slice of cucumber lengthways, about 7.5 cm/3 in long, avoiding the seeds. Remove any skin and cut into strips to within 1 cm/½ in from the end. Remove alternate strips.

2 Carefully bend the strips towards the uncut end, tucking them in so that they stay securely in place. Leave to soak in iced water until required and pat dry before use.

SPRING ONION BRUSH

1 Trim the green part of a spring onion and remove the base of the bulb – you should be left with a piece about 7.5 cm/3 in long. Make a lengthways cut about 2.5 cm/1 in long at one end of the spring onion.

2 Roll the spring onion through 90° and cut again. Repeat this process at the other end. Place in iced water until the shreds open out and curl. Pat dry with kitchen paper before use.

Spice Mixtures and Stocks

Use these spice mixtures to add heat and flavour to Thai curries, fish cakes and Balti dishes. They are quick and easy to make, but you can buy them ready-made from larger supermarkets.

THAI RED CURRY PASTE

INGREDIENTS
4 fresh red chillies
2.5 cm/1 in piece fresh root
  ginger
4 shallots
4-6 garlic cloves
4 lemon grass stalks
20 ml/4 tsp coriander seeds
10 ml/2 tsp cumin seeds
20 ml/2 tsp hot paprika
1.5 ml/¼ tsp ground turmeric
2.5 ml/½ tsp salt
grated rind and juice of 2 limes
15 ml/1 tbsp vegetable oil

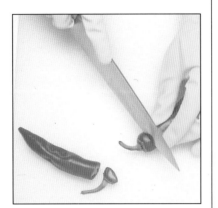

1 Peel and chop the ginger, shallots and garlic. Peel and finely chop the lemon grass. Wearing rubber gloves, remove the stalks from the chillies, then cut them in half lengthways. Scrape out the seeds and fleshy white ribs, then roughly chop the flesh.

THAI GREEN CURRY PASTE

INGREDIENTS
6 spring onions
4 fresh coriander stems, washed
4 kaffir lime leaves
6-8 fresh green chillies
4 garlic cloves, chopped
2.5 cm/1 in piece fresh root
  ginger, chopped
1 lemon grass stalk, chopped
45 ml/3 tbsp chopped fresh
  coriander
45 ml/3 tbsp chopped fresh basil
15 ml/1 tbsp vegetable oil

2 Heat a small frying pan over a medium heat, then add the coriander and cumin seeds. Toss them in the pan until the spices turn a shade darker and emit a roasted aroma. Leave to cool.

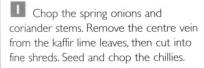

3 Place all the ingredients in a blender or food processor and process to form a smooth paste. Store in a screw-top jar for up to 1 month in the fridge and use as required.

1 Chop the spring onions and coriander stems. Remove the centre vein from the kaffir lime leaves, then cut into fine shreds. Seed and chop the chillies.

2 Put all the ingredients in a blender or food processor and process to form a smooth paste. Store in a screw-top jar for up to 2 weeks in the fridge and use as required.

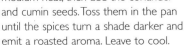

GARAM MASALA

INGREDIENTS
7.5 cm/3 in piece cinnamon stick
2 bay leaves
5 ml/1 tsp cumin seeds
5 ml/1 tsp whole cloves
5 ml/1 tsp black peppercorns
¼ nutmeg, grated

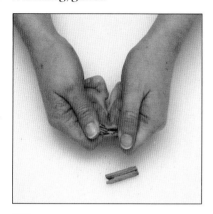

1 Break the cinnamon stick into pieces. Crumble the bay leaves.

2 Heat a small frying pan over a medium heat, then add the bay leaves and all the spices except the nutmeg. Dry-roast until the spices turn a shade darker and emit a roasted aroma, stirring or shaking the pan frequently to prevent burning. Leave to cool. Place all the ingredients in a spice mill or electric coffee grinder and grind to a fine powder. Store in a small jar with a tight-fitting lid for up to 2 months.

CHICKEN STOCK

INGREDIENTS
1 kg/2¼ lb uncooked chicken bones, such as backs, wings etc.
500 g/1¼ lb chicken pieces
2.4 litres/4 pints/10 cups water
2 thin slices fresh root ginger
2 spring onions, white parts only
2 unpeeled garlic cloves
salt, to taste

1 Place all the ingredients except the salt in a large pan and bring to a simmer. Skim off any scum. Simmer for 3–4 hours to extract all the flavour. Season with salt to taste.

2 Strain the stock, pressing the solid ingredients with the back of a ladle or spoon to extract all the liquid. Allow the stock to cool, then chill. Spoon off the fat from the surface. Use as required.

FRESH COCONUT MILK

INGREDIENTS
grated fresh coconut to fill a measuring jug to the 400 ml/14 fl oz/1⅔ cups mark
300ml/½ pint/1¼ cups hot water

1 First you will need to break open a fresh coconut. To do this, push a skewer into the three holes in the top of the coconut and drain out the liquid. Place the coconut in a plastic bag and hit it hard with a hammer. To remove the outer shell from the coconut pieces, prise the tip of a small sharp knife between it and the coconut flesh. Remove the inner brown skin using a potato peeler. Grate the flesh.

2 Put the measured grated coconut and hot water into a blender or food processor fitted with a metal blade and process for 1 minute. Strain the coconut mixture through a sieve lined with muslin into a bowl, gathering up the corners of the cloth and squeezing out the liquid. The coconut milk is now ready; stir before use.

left to right:
chicken stock
garam masala
fresh coconut milk

General Rules for Stir-frying

Stir-frying takes very little actual cooking time, often no more than a matter of minutes. For this reason it is important that all the ingredients are prepared ahead of time – washed, peeled or grated as required, and cut to approximately the same shape and size, to ensure even cooking.

1 Always heat the wok (or frying pan, if using) for a few minutes before adding the oil or any other ingredients.

2 If adding oil, swirl the oil into the wok and allow it to heat up before adding the next ingredients.

3 When adding the first ingredients, reduce the heat a little. This will ensure they are not overcooked or burnt by the time the remaining ingredients have been added to the wok.

4 Once all the ingredients have been added, quickly increase the heat, as this will allow the dish to cook in the least possible time. This allows the ingredients to retain a crisp, fresh texture, and prevents them from becoming soggy or laden with oil.

5 Use a long handled scoop or spatula to turn the ingredients as you stir-fry. This will allow the ingredients to cook evenly and quickly.

6 It may be easier to slice meat for stir-frying if it has been frozen slightly for an hour or so. By the time you have sliced it, the meat will be thawed to cook.

Slicing Onions

Stir-fry onion slices with the main vegetables. Ensure they are all cut to the same size for even cooking.

1 Peel the onion. Cut in half with a large knife and set it cut-side down on to a chopping board.

2 Cut out a triangular piece of the core from each half.

3 Cut across each half in vertical slices.

Chopping Onions

Diced onions can be used to flavour oil before stir-frying the main ingredients.

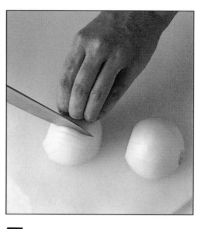

1 Peel the onion. Cut in half with a knife and set it cut-side down on a board. Make lengthwise vertical cuts along the onion, cutting almost through to the root.

2 Make 2 horizontal cuts from the stalk and towards the root, but not through it.

3 Cut the onion crosswise to form small dice.

Mini Spring Rolls

Eat these light crispy parcels with your fingers. If you like slightly spicier food, sprinkle them with a little cayenne pepper before serving.

Makes 20

INGREDIENTS
1 green chilli
125 ml/4 fl oz/½ cup vegetable oil
1 small onion, finely chopped
1 clove garlic, crushed
75 g/3 oz cooked chicken breast
1 small carrot, cut into fine
　matchsticks
1 spring onion, finely sliced
1 small red pepper, seeded and cut
　into fine matchsticks
25 g/1 oz beansprouts
5 ml/1 tsp sesame oil
4 large sheets filo pastry
1 × size 4 egg white, lightly beaten
long chives, to garnish (optional)
45 ml/3 tbsp light soy sauce, to serve

spring onions

chilli

pepper

garlic

beansprouts

COOK'S TIP

Be careful to avoid touching your face or eyes when deseeding and chopping chillies because they are very potent and may cause burning and irritation to the skin. Try preparing chillies under running water.

1 Carefully remove the seeds from the chilli and chop finely, wearing rubber gloves to protect your hands, if necessary.

2 Heat the wok, then add 30 ml/2 tbsp of the vegetable oil. When hot, add the onion, garlic and chilli. Stir-fry for 1 minute.

3 Slice the chicken thinly, then add to the wok and fry over a high heat, stirring constantly until browned.

4 Add the carrot, spring onion and red pepper and stir-fry for 2 minutes. Add the beansprouts, stir in the sesame oil and leave to cool.

COOK'S TIP

Always keep filo pastry sheets covered with a dry, clean cloth until needed, to prevent them drying out.

5 Cut each sheet of filo into 5 short strips. Place a small amount of filling at one end of each strip, then fold in the long sides and roll up the pastry. Seal and glaze the parcels with the egg white, then chill uncovered for 15 minutes before frying.

6 Wipe out the wok with kitchen towels, heat it, and add the remaining vegetable oil. When the oil is hot, fry the rolls in batches until crisp and golden brown. Drain on kitchen towels and serve dipped in light soy sauce.

Lettuce-wrapped Garlic Lamb

For this tasty starter lamb is stir-fried with garlic, ginger and spices, then served in crisp lettuce leaves with yogurt, a dab of lime pickle and mint leaves – the contrast of hot and spicy and cool and crisp is excellent.

Serves 4

INGREDIENTS
450 g/1 lb lamb neck fillet
2.5 ml/½ tsp chilli powder
10 ml/2 tsp ground coriander
5 ml/1 tsp ground cumin
2.5 ml/½ tsp ground turmeric
30 ml/2 tbsp groundnut oil
3–4 garlic cloves, chopped
15 ml/1 tbsp grated fresh
  root ginger
150 ml/¼ pint/⅔ cup lamb
  stock or water
4–6 spring onions, sliced
30 ml/2 tbsp chopped
  fresh coriander
15 ml/1 tbsp lemon juice
lettuce leaves, yogurt, lime pickle
  and mint leaves, to serve

coriander

stock

garlic

lamb

ginger

groundnut oil

spring onions

VARIATION
Vegetables, such as cooked diced potatoes or peas, can be added to the mince.

1 Trim the lamb fillet of any fat and cube in to small pieces, then mince in a blender or food processor, taking care not to over-process.

2 In a bowl mix together the chilli powder, ground coriander, cumin and turmeric. Add the lamb and rub the spice mixture into the meat. Cover and leave to marinate for about 1 hour.

3 Heat a wok until hot. Add the oil and swirl it around. When hot, add the garlic and ginger and allow to sizzle for a few seconds.

4 Add the lamb and continue to stir-fry for 2–3 minutes.

5 Pour in the stock and continue to stir-fry until all the stock has been absorbed and the lamb is tender, adding more stock if necessary.

6 Add the spring onions, fresh coriander and lemon juice, then stir-fry for a further 30–45 seconds. Serve at once with the lettuce leaves, yogurt, pickle and mint leaves.

Crispy "Seaweed" with Flaked Almonds

This popular starter in Chinese restaurants is in fact usually made not with seaweed but spring greens! It is easy to make at home and the result is delicious.

Serves 4-6

INGREDIENTS
450 g/1 lb spring greens
groundnut oil, for deep-frying
1.5 ml/¼ tsp sea salt flakes
5 ml/1 tsp caster sugar
50 g/2 oz/½ cup flaked
   almonds, toasted

spring greens

almonds

groundnut oil

sea salt

sugar

COOK'S TIP
It is important to dry the spring greens thoroughly before deep-frying them, otherwise it will be difficult to achieve the desired crispness without destroying their vivid colour.

1 Wash the spring greens under cold running water and pat well with kitchen paper to dry thoroughly. Remove and discard the thick white stalks from the spring greens.

2 Lay several leaves on top of one another, roll up tightly and, using a sharp knife, slice as finely as possible into thread-like strips.

3 Half-fill a wok with oil and heat to 180°C/350°F. Deep fry the spring greens in batches for about 1 minute until they darken and crisp. Remove each batch from the wok as soon as it is ready and drain on kitchen paper.

4 Transfer the "seaweed" to a serving dish, sprinkle with the salt and sugar, then mix well. Garnish with the toasted flaked almonds scattered over.

Sesame Seed Chicken Bites

Best served warm, these crunchy bites are delicious accompanied by a glass of chilled dry white wine.

Makes 20

INGREDIENTS
175 g/6 oz raw chicken breast
2 cloves garlic, crushed
2.5 cm/1 in piece root ginger, peeled
    and grated
1 × size 4 egg white
5 ml/1 tsp cornflour
25 g/1 oz/¼ cup shelled pistachios,
    roughly chopped
60 ml/4 tbsp sesame seeds
30 ml/2 tbsp grapeseed oil
salt and freshly ground black pepper

FOR THE SAUCE
45 ml/3 tbsp/¼ cup hoisin sauce
15 ml/1 tbsp sweet chilli sauce

TO GARNISH
root ginger, finely shredded
pistachios, roughly chopped
fresh dill sprigs

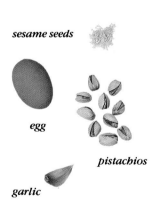

sesame seeds

egg

pistachios

garlic

ginger

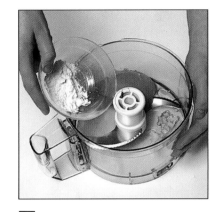

1 Place the chicken, garlic, grated ginger, egg white and cornflour into the food processor and process them to a smooth paste.

2 Stir in the pistachios and season well with salt and pepper.

3 Roll into 20 balls and coat with sesame seeds. Heat the wok and add the oil. When the oil is hot, stir-fry the chicken bites in batches, turning regularly until golden. Drain on kitchen towels.

4 Make the sauce by mixing together the hoisin and chilli sauces in a bowl. Garnish the bites with shredded ginger, pistachios and dill, then serve hot, with a dish of sauce for dipping.

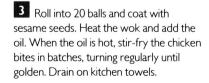

Mixed Spiced Nuts

These make an excellent accompaniment to drinks. They will store for up to a month in an air-tight container if they are not mixed together.

Serves 4–6

INGREDIENTS

75 g/3 oz dried unsweetened
  coconut flakes
75 ml/5 tbsp peanut oil
2.5 ml/½ tsp chilli powder
5 ml/1 tsp ground paprika
5 ml/1 tsp tomato purée
225 g/8 oz/2 cups unsalted cashews
225 g/8 oz/2 cups whole blanched
  almonds
60 ml/4 tbsp caster sugar
5 ml/1 tsp ground cumin
2.5 ml/½ tsp salt
freshly ground black pepper
mustard and cress, to garnish

cashews

paprika

chilli powder

cumin

almonds

I Heat the wok, add the coconut flakes and dry-fry until golden. Leave to cool.

2 Heat the wok and add 45 ml/3 tbsp of the peanut oil. When the oil is hot, add the chilli, paprika and tomato purée. Gently stir-fry the cashews in the spicy mix until well coated. Drain well and season. Leave to cool.

3 Wipe out the wok with kitchen towels, heat it, then add the remaining oil. When the oil is hot, add the almonds and sprinkle in the sugar. Stir-fry gently until the almonds are golden brown and the sugar is caramelized. Place the cumin and salt in a bowl. Add the almonds, toss well, then leave to cool.

4 Mix the cashews, almonds and coconut flakes together, garnish with mustard and cress and serve with drinks.

Thai Fish Cakes

Bursting with the flavours of chillies, lime and lemon grass, these little fish cakes make a wonderful starter.

Serves 4

INGREDIENTS
450 g/1 lb white fish fillets, such as cod or haddock
3 spring onions, sliced
30 ml/2 tbsp chopped fresh coriander
30 ml/2 tbsp Thai red curry paste
1 fresh green chilli, seeded and chopped
10 ml/2 tsp grated lime rind
15 ml/1 tbsp lime juice
30 ml/2 tbsp groundnut oil
salt, to taste
crisp lettuce leaves, shredded spring onions, fresh red chilli slices, coriander sprigs and lime wedges, to serve

lettuce   *white fish fillets*

lime   *spring onions*

groundnut oil

coriander

red chilli

green chilli   *Thai red curry paste*

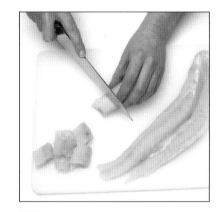

1 Cut the fish into chunks, then place in a blender or food processor.

2 Add the spring onions, coriander, red curry paste, green chilli, lime rind and juice to the fish. Season with salt. Process until finely minced.

3 Using lightly floured hands, divide the mixture into 16 pieces and shape each one into a small cake about 4 cm/1½ in across. Place the fish cakes on a plate, cover with clear film and chill for about 2 hours until firm. Heat the wok over a high heat until hot. Add the oil and swirl it around.

4 Fry the fish cakes, a few at a time, for 6–8 minutes, turning them carefully until evenly browned. Drain each batch on kitchen paper and keep hot while cooking the remainder. Serve on a bed of crisp lettuce leaves with shredded spring onions, red chilli slices, coriander sprigs and lime wedges.

Chinese Spiced Salt Spareribs

Fragrant with spices, this authentic Chinese dish makes a great starter to an informal meal. Don't forget the finger bowls!

Serves 4

INGREDIENTS
675–900 g/1½–2 lb meaty
  pork spareribs
25 ml/1½ tbsp cornflour
groundnut oil, for deep frying
coriander sprigs, to garnish

FOR THE SPICED SALT
5 ml/1 tsp Szechuan peppercorns
30 ml/2 tbsp coarse sea salt
2.5 ml/½ tsp Chinese five-
  spice powder

FOR THE MARINADE
30 ml/2 tbsp light soy sauce
5 ml/1 tsp caster sugar
15 ml/1 tbsp Chinese rice wine
ground black pepper

Chinese rice wine

pork spareribs

Szechuan peppercorns

Chinese five-spice powder

coriander

light soy sauce

groundnut oil

sea salt

1 Using a heavy sharp cleaver, chop the spareribs into pieces about 5 cm/ 2 in long or ask your butcher to do this, then place them in a shallow dish.

2 To make the spiced salt, heat a wok to a medium heat. Add the Szechuan peppercorns and salt and dry fry for about 3 minutes, stirring constantly until the mixture colours slightly. Remove from the heat and stir in the five-spice powder. Leave to cool.

3 Using a mortar and pestle or an electric coffee grinder, grind the spiced salt to a fine powder.

4 Sprinkle 5 ml/1 tsp of the spiced salt over the spareribs and rub in well with your hands. Add the soy sauce, sugar, rice wine or sherry and some freshly ground black pepper, then toss the ribs in the marinade until well coated. Cover and leave to marinate in the fridge for about 2 hours, turning the spareribs occasionally.

COOK'S TIP
Any leftover spiced salt can be kept for several months in a screw-top jar. Use to rub on the flesh of duck, chicken or pork before cooking.

5 Pour off any excess marinade from the spareribs. Sprinkle the pieces with cornflour and mix well to coat evenly.

6 Half-fill a wok with oil and heat to 180°C/350°F. Deep fry the spareribs in batches for 3 minutes until pale golden. Remove and set aside. Reheat the oil to the same temperature. Return the spareribs to the oil and deep-fry for a second time for 1–2 minutes until crisp and thoroughly cooked. Drain on kitchen paper. Transfer the ribs to a warmed serving platter and sprinkle over 5–7.5 ml/1–1½ tsp spiced salt. Garnish with coriander sprigs.

Butterfly Prawns

Use raw prawns if you can because the flavour will be better, but if you substitute cooked prawns, cut down the stir-fry cooking time by one third.

Serves 4

INGREDIENTS
2.5 cm/1 in piece root ginger
350 g/12 oz raw prawns, thawed if
    frozen
50 g/2 oz/½ cup raw peanuts, roughly
    chopped
45 ml/3 tbsp vegetable oil
1 clove garlic, crushed
1 red chilli, finely chopped
45 ml/3 tbsp smooth peanut butter
15 ml/1 tbsp fresh coriander, chopped
fresh coriander sprigs, to garnish

FOR THE DRESSING
150 ml/¼ pint/⅔ cup natural
    low-fat yogurt
5 cm/2 in piece cucumber, diced
salt and freshly ground black pepper

diced
cucumber

peanuts

prawn

coriander

chilli

1 To make the dressing, mix together the yogurt, cucumber and seasoning in a bowl, then leave to chill while preparing and cooking the prawns.

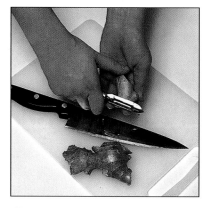

2 Peel the ginger, and chop it finely.

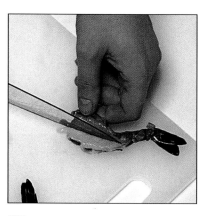

3 Prepare the prawns by peeling off the shells, leaving the tails intact. Make a slit down the back of each prawn and remove the black vein, then slit the prawn completely down the back and open it out to make a 'butterfly'.

4 Heat the wok and dry-fry the peanuts, stirring constantly until golden brown. Leave to cool. Wipe out the wok with kitchen towels.

5 Heat the wok, add the oil and when hot add the ginger, garlic and chilli. Stir-fry for 2–3 minutes until the garlic is softened but not brown.

6 Add the prawns, then increase the heat and stir-fry for 1–2 minutes until the prawns turn pink. Stir in the peanut butter and stir-fry for 2 minutes. Add the chopped coriander, then scatter in the peanuts. Garnish with coriander sprigs and serve with the cucumber dressing.

Steamed Spiced Pork and Water Chestnut Wontons

Ginger and Chinese five-spice powder flavour this version of steamed open dumplings – a favourite snack in many teahouses.

Makes about 36

INGREDIENTS

2 large Chinese cabbage leaves, plus extra for lining the steamer
2 spring onions, finely chopped
1 cm/½ in piece fresh root ginger, finely chopped
50 g/2oz canned water chestnuts (drained weight), rinsed and finely chopped
225 g/8oz minced pork
2.5 ml/½ tsp Chinese five-spice powder
15 ml/1 tbsp cornflour
15 ml/1 tbsp light soy sauce
15 ml/1 tbsp Chinese rice wine
10 ml/2 tsp sesame oil
generous pinch of caster sugar
about 36 wonton wrappers, each 7.5 cm/3 in square
light soy sauce and hot chilli oil, for dipping

caster sugar

Chinese cabbage

light soy sauce

spring onions

sesame oil

cornflour

wonton wrappers

water chestnuts

pork

Chinese five-spice powder

Chinese rice wine

ginger

VARIATION

These can also be deep fried, in which case fold the edges over the filling to enclose it completely. Press well to seal. Deep fry in batches in hot oil for about 2 minutes.

1 Place the Chinese cabbage leaves one on top of another. Cut them lengthways into quarters and then across into thin shreds.

2 Place the shredded Chinese cabbage leaves in a bowl. Add the spring onions, ginger, water chestnuts, pork, five-spice powder, cornflour, soy sauce, rice wine, sesame oil and sugar; mix well.

3 Set one wonton wrapper on a work surface. Place a heaped teaspoon of the filling in the centre of the wrapper, then lightly dampen the edges with water.

4 Lift the wrapper up around the filling, gathering to form a purse. Squeeze the wrapper firmly around the middle, then tap on the bottom to make a flat base. The top should be open. Place the wonton on a tray and cover with a damp dish towel.

5 Line the steamer with cabbage leaves and steam the dumplings for 12–15 minutes until tender. Remove each batch from the steamer as soon as they are cooked, cover with foil and keep warm. Serve hot with soy sauce and chilli oil for dipping.

Stir-fried Potatoes and Eggs

A bacon and egg breakfast dish done in true stir-fry style – fast and flavourful.

Serves 4

INGREDIENTS
350 g/12 oz cooked potatoes
45 ml/3 tbsp olive oil
10 ml/2 tsp fresh rosemary, chopped
pinch of freshly grated nutmeg
75 g/3 oz smoked bacon, cut
    into cubes
4 quail's eggs
salt flakes and freshly ground
    black pepper
fresh rosemary sprigs, to garnish

rosemary

*smoked
bacon*

quail's eggs

potato

1 Coarsely grate the potatoes and thoroughly pat dry on kitchen towels to remove all the moisture.

2 Heat the wok, then add 30 ml/2 tbsp of oil. When the oil is hot, add the potatoes and cook them in batches until crisp and golden. This will take about 10 minutes. Drain them on kitchen towels, mix with the rosemary, nutmeg and seasoning and keep warm.

3 Add the bacon to the hot wok and stir-fry until crisp. Sprinkle the bacon on top of the potato, then season well.

4 Heat the wok, then add the remaining oil. When the oil is hot, fry the quail's eggs for about 2 minutes. Make a pile of the rosemary rosti, season it well, garnish with sprigs of fresh rosemary, then serve with the eggs.

Sweetcorn and Chicken Soup

This popular classic Chinese soup is delicious, and very easy to make.

Serves 4-6

INGREDIENTS

1 chicken breast fillet, about
   115 g/4 oz, cubed
10 ml/2 tsp light soy sauce
15 ml/1 tbsp Chinese rice wine
5 ml/1 tsp cornflour
60 ml/4 tbsp cold water
5 ml/1 tsp sesame oil
30 ml/2 tbsp groundnut oil
5 ml/1 tsp grated fresh root
   ginger
1 litre/1¾ pints/4 cups chicken
   stock
425 g/15 oz can cream-style
   sweetcorn
225 g/8 oz can sweetcorn kernels
2 eggs, beaten
2-3 spring onions, green parts
   only, cut into tiny rounds
salt and ground black pepper

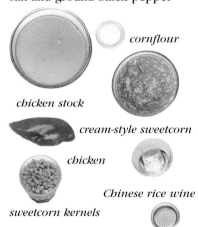

cornflour

chicken stock

cream-style sweetcorn

chicken

Chinese rice wine

sweetcorn kernels

egg

sesame oil

ginger

1 Mince the chicken in a food processor, taking care not to over-process. Transfer the chicken to a bowl and stir in the soy sauce, rice wine, cornflour, water, sesame oil and seasoning. Cover and leave for about 15 minutes to absorb the flavours.

2 Heat a wok over a medium heat. Add the groundnut oil and swirl it around. Add the ginger and stir-fry for a few seconds. Add the stock, creamed sweetcorn and sweetcorn kernels. Bring to just below boiling point.

3 Spoon about 90 ml/6 tbsp of the hot liquid into the chicken mixture until it forms a smooth paste and stir. Return to the wok. Slowly bring to the boil, stirring constantly, then simmer for 2–3 minutes until cooked.

4 Pour the beaten eggs into the soup in a slow steady stream, using a fork or chopsticks to stir the top of the soup in a figure-of-eight pattern. The egg should set in lacy shreds. Serve immediately with the spring onions sprinkled over.

Vegetable Tempura

These deep-fried fritters are based on Kaki-age, a Japanese dish that often incorporates fish and prawns as well as vegetables.

COOK'S TIP
Paring strips of peel from the courgettes and aubergine will avoid too much tough skin in the finished dish.

Makes 8

INGREDIENTS
2 medium courgettes
½ medium aubergine
1 large carrot
½ small Spanish onion
1 egg
120 ml/4 fl oz/½ cup
   iced water
115 g/4 oz/1 cup plain flour
salt and ground black pepper
vegetable oil, for deep-frying
sea salt flakes, lemon slices and
   Japanese soy sauce (*shoyu*),
   to serve

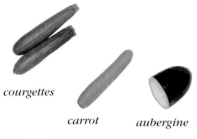
courgettes

carrot   *aubergine*

Spanish onion

plain flour

egg
          vegetable oil

1 Using a potato peeler, pare strips of peel from the courgettes and aubergine to give a stripy effect.

2 Cut the courgettes, aubergine and carrot into strips about 7.5–10 cm/ 3–4 in long and 3 mm/⅛ in wide.

3 Put the courgettes, aubergine and carrot in a colander and sprinkle liberally with salt. Leave for about 30 minutes, then rinse thoroughly under cold running water. Drain well.

4 Thinly slice the onion from top to base, discarding the plump pieces in the middle. Separate the layers so that there are lots of fine long strips. Mix all the vegetables together and season with salt and pepper.

5 Make the batter immediately before frying: mix the egg and iced water in a bowl, then sift in the flour. Mix very briefly using a fork or chopsticks. Do not overmix – the batter should remain lumpy. Add the vegetables to the batter and mix to combine.

6 Meanwhile, half-fill a wok with oil and heat to 180°C/350°F. Scoop up one heaped tablespoon of the mixture at a time and carefully lower into the oil. Deep fry in batches for about 3 minutes until golden brown and crisp. Drain on kitchen paper. Serve each diner with salt, lemon slices and a tiny bowl of Japanese soy sauce for dipping.

Crispy Spring Rolls with Sweet Chilli Dipping Sauce

Miniature spring rolls make delicious starters or party finger food.

Makes 20-24

INGREDIENTS
25 g/1 oz rice vermicelli noodles
groundnut oil
5 ml/1 tsp grated fresh
   root ginger
2 spring onions, finely shredded
50 g/2 oz carrot, finely shredded
50 g/2 oz mange-touts, shredded
25 g/1 oz young spinach leaves
50 g/2 oz fresh beansprouts
15 ml/1 tbsp chopped fresh mint
15 ml/1 tbsp chopped
   fresh coriander
30 ml/2 tbsp Thai fish sauce
   (*nam pla*)
20-24 spring roll wrappers, each
   13 cm/5 in square
1 egg white, lightly beaten

FOR THE DIPPING SAUCE
50 g/2 oz/4 tbsp caster sugar
50 ml/2 fl oz/¼ cup rice vinegar
2 fresh red chillies, seeded and
   finely chopped

noodles
spinach
spring onions
spring roll wrappers
Thai fish sauce

beansprouts

ginger
mange-touts
carrot

1 First make the dipping sauce: place the sugar and vinegar in a small pan with 30 ml/2 tbsp water. Heat gently, stirring until the sugar dissolves, then boil rapidly until it forms a light syrup. Stir in the chillies and leave to cool.

2 Soak the noodles according to the packet instructions; rinse and drain well. Using scissors, snip the noodles into short lengths.

3 Heat a wok until hot. Add 15 ml/ 1 tbsp oil and swirl it around. Add the ginger and spring onions and stir-fry for 15 seconds. Add the carrot and mange-touts and stir-fry for 2–3 minutes. Add the spinach, beansprouts, mint, coriander, fish sauce and noodles and stir-fry for a further minute. Set aside to cool.

4 Take one spring roll wrapper and arrange it so that it faces you in a diamond shape. Place a spoonful of filling just below the centre, then fold up the bottom point over the filling.

5 Fold in each side, then roll up tightly. Brush the end with beaten egg white to seal. Repeat until all the filling has been used.

6 Half-fill a wok with oil and heat to 180°C/350°F. Deep fry the spring rolls in batches for 3–4 minutes until golden and crisp. Drain on kitchen paper. Serve hot with the sweet chilli dipping sauce.

COOK'S TIP
You can cook the spring rolls 2–3 hours in advance, then reheat them on a foil-lined baking sheet at 200°C/400°F/Gas 6 for about 10 minutes.

Quick-fried Prawns with Hot Spices

These spicy prawns that cook in moments make a wonderful starter. Don't forget to provide your guests with finger bowls.

Serves 4

INGREDIENTS
450 g/1 lb large raw prawns
2.5 cm/1 in piece fresh root ginger, grated
2 garlic cloves, crushed
5 ml/1 tsp hot chilli powder
5 ml/1 tsp ground turmeric
10 ml/2 tsp black mustard seeds
seeds from 4 green cardamom pods, crushed
50 g/2 oz/4 tbsp ghee or butter
120 ml/4fl oz/½ cup coconut milk
30–45 ml/2–3 tbsp chopped fresh coriander
salt and ground black pepper
naan bread, to serve

prawns

coriander

coconut milk

chilli powder

ghee

black mustard seeds

turmeric

ginger

garlic

cardamom pods

COOK'S TIP
If raw prawns are unavailable, use cooked ones instead, but simmer gently in the coconut milk for just 1–2 minutes.

1 Peel the prawns carefully, leaving the tails attached.

2 Using a small sharp knife, make a slit along the back of each prawn and remove the dark vein. Rinse under cold running water, drain and pat dry.

3 Put the ginger, garlic, chilli powder, turmeric, mustard seeds and cardamom seeds in a bowl. Add the prawns and toss to coat with the spice mixture.

4 Heat a karahi or wok until hot. Add the ghee or butter and swirl it around until foaming.

5 Add the marinated prawns and stir-fry for 1–1½ minutes until they are just turning pink.

6 Stir in the coconut milk and simmer for 3–4 minutes until the prawns are cooked through. Season with salt and pepper. Sprinkle over the coriander and serve at once with naan bread.

Prawn Toasts

These crunchy sesame-topped toasts are simple to prepare using a food processor for the prawn paste.

Makes 64

INGREDIENTS
225 g/8 oz cooked, shelled prawns,
    well drained and dried
1 egg white
2 spring onions, chopped
5 ml/1 tsp chopped fresh root ginger
1 garlic clove, chopped
5 ml/1 tsp cornflour
2.5 ml/½ tsp salt
2.5 ml/½ tsp sugar
2–3 dashes hot pepper sauce
8 slices firm textured white bread
60–75 ml/4–5 tbsp sesame seeds
vegetable oil, for frying
spring onion pompom, to garnish

bread

vegetable oil

egg white

sesame seeds

root ginger

sugar

prawns

garlic

cornflour

hot pepper sauce

spring onions

1 Put the first 9 ingredients in the bowl of a food processor and process until the mixture forms a smooth paste, scraping down the side of the bowl occasionally.

2 Spread the prawn paste evenly over the bread slices, then sprinkle over the sesame seeds, pressing to make them stick. Remove the crusts, then cut each slice diagonally into 4 triangles, then cut each in half again to make 64 in total.

3 Heat 5 cm/2 in vegetable oil in a heavy saucepan or wok, until hot but not smoking. Fry the prawn-coated triangles for 30–60 seconds, turning once. Drain on paper towels and serve hot.

COOK'S TIP

You can prepare these in advance and heat them up in a hot oven before serving. Make sure they are crisp and properly heated through though, they won't be nearly as enjoyable if there's no crunch!

Thai-fried Vegetables in Wonton Cups

These crispy cups are an ideal way to serve stir-fried vegetables; use your imagination to vary the fillings.

Makes 24

INGREDIENTS

30 ml/2 tbsp vegetable oil, plus extra
    for greasing
24 small wonton wrappers
120 ml/4 fl oz/½ cup Hoi Sin sauce or
    plum sauce (optional)
5 ml/1 tsp sesame oil
1 garlic clove, finely chopped
1 cm/½ in piece fresh root ginger,
    finely chopped
5 cm/2 in piece of lemon grass,
    crushed
6–8 asparagus spears, cut into 3 cm/
    1¼ in pieces
8–10 baby sweetcorn, cut in half
    lengthways
1 small red pepper, seeded and cut
    into short slivers
15–30 ml/1–2 tbsp sugar
30 ml/2 tbsp soy sauce
juice of 1 lime
5–10 ml/1–2 tsp Chinese-style chilli
    sauce (or to taste)
1 tsp *buac nam* or Thai or other fish
    sauce

lemon grass

red pepper

Hoi Sin sauce

wonton wrappers

baby sweetcorn

vegetable oil

asparagus

sesame oil

soy sauce

lime

garlic

3 Add the sugar, soy sauce, lime juice, chilli sauce and fish sauce and toss well to coat. Stir-fry for 30 seconds longer.

4 Spoon an equal amount of vegetable mixture into each of the prepared wonton cups and serve hot.

1 Preheat the oven to 180°C/350°F/ Gas 4. Lightly grease 24 4 cm/1½ in bun tins. Press 1 wonton wrapper into each cup, turning the edges up to form a cup shape. Bake for 8–10 minutes, until crisp and golden. Carefully remove to a wire rack to cool. If you like, brush each cup with a little Hoi Sin or plum sauce (this will help keep the cups crisp if preparing them in advance).

2 In a wok or large frying pan, heat 30 ml/2 tbsp vegetable oil and the sesame oil until very hot. Add the garlic, ginger and lemon grass and stir-fry for 15 seconds until fragrant. Add the asparagus, sweetcorn and red pepper pieces and stir-fry for 2 minutes until tender crisp.

Hot Spicy Crab Claws

Crab claws are used to delicious effect in this quick starter based on an Indonesian dish called *Kepiting Pedas*.

Serves 4

INGREDIENTS
12 fresh or frozen and thawed
   cooked crab claws
4 shallots, roughly chopped
2-4 fresh red chillies, seeded and
   roughly chopped
3 garlic cloves, roughly chopped
5 ml/1 tsp grated fresh
   root ginger
2.5 ml/½ tsp ground coriander
45 ml/3 tbsp groundnut oil
60 ml/4 tbsp water
10 ml/2 tsp sweet soy sauce
   (*kecap manis*)
10-15 ml/2-3 tsp lime juice
salt, to taste

shallots

crab claws

sweet soy sauce

coriander

garlic

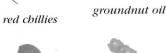
red chillies

groundnut oil

lime

ginger

1 Crack the crab claws with the back of a heavy knife to make eating easier. Set aside. In a mortar, pound the chopped shallots with the pestle until pulpy. Add the chillies, garlic, ginger and ground coriander and pound until the mixture forms a coarse paste.

2 Heat the wok over a medium heat. Add the oil and swirl it around. When it is hot, stir in the chilli paste. Stir-fry for about 30 seconds. Increase the heat to high. Add the crab claws and stir-fry for another 3–4 minutes.

3 Stir in the water, sweet soy sauce, lime juice and salt to taste. Continue to stir-fry for 1–2 minutes. Serve at once, garnished with fresh coriander. The crab claws are eaten with the fingers, so provide finger bowls.

COOK'S TIP
If whole crab claws are unavailable look out for frozen ready-prepared crab claws. These are shelled with just the tip of the claw attached to the white meat. Stir fry for about two minutes until hot through.

Thai Seafood Salad

This seafood salad with chilli, lemon grass and fish sauce is light and refreshing.

Serves 4

INGREDIENTS
225 g/8 oz ready-prepared squid
225 g/8 oz raw tiger prawns
8 scallops, shelled
225 g/8 oz firm white fish
30–45 ml/2–3 tbsp olive oil
small mixed lettuce leaves and
   coriander sprigs, to serve

FOR THE DRESSING
2 small fresh red chillies, seeded
   and finely chopped
5 cm/2 in piece lemon grass,
   finely chopped
2 fresh kaffir lime leaves,
   shredded
30 ml/2 tbsp Thai fish sauce
   (*nam pla*)
2 shallots, thinly sliced
30 ml/2 tbsp lime juice
30 ml/2 tbsp rice vinegar
10 ml/2 tsp caster sugar

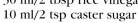

white fish   *squid*

scallops
tiger prawns

lemon grass

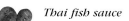

Thai fish sauce

shallots   *kaffir lime leaves*

1 Prepare the seafood: slit open the squid bodies, score the flesh with a sharp knife, then cut into square pieces. Halve the tentacles, if necessary. Peel and devein the prawns. Remove the dark beard-like fringe and tough muscle from the scallops. Cube the white fish.

2 Heat a wok until hot. Add the oil and swirl it around, then add the prawns and stir-fry for 2–3 minutes until pink. Transfer to a large bowl. Stir-fry the squid and scallops for 1–2 minutes until opaque. Remove and add to the prawns. Stir-fry the white fish for 2–3 minutes. Remove and add to the cooked seafood. Reserve any juices.

3 Put all the dressing ingredients in a small bowl with the reserved juices from the wok; mix well.

4 Pour the dressing over the seafood and toss gently. Arrange the salad leaves and coriander sprigs on four individual plates, then spoon the seafood on top. Serve at once.

Salmon Teriyaki

Marinating the salmon makes it so wonderfully tender, it just melts in the mouth, and the crunchy condiment provides an excellent foil. If you are short of time, you can buy good ready-made teriyaki sauce in a bottle.

Serves 4

INGREDIENTS
675 g/1½ lb salmon fillet
5 ml/1 tsp salt
30 ml/2 tbsp sunflower oil
watercress, to garnish

FOR THE TERIYAKI SAUCE
5 ml/1 tsp caster sugar
5 ml/1 tsp dry white wine
5 ml/1 tsp rice wine or dry sherry
30 ml/2 tbsp dark soy sauce

FOR THE CONDIMENT
5 cm/2 in piece root ginger, peeled
  and grated
few drops of pink food colouring
50 g/2 oz mooli, grated

salmon

watercress

soy sauce

mooli

ginger

1 Mix all the teriyaki sauce ingredients together until the sugar dissolves.

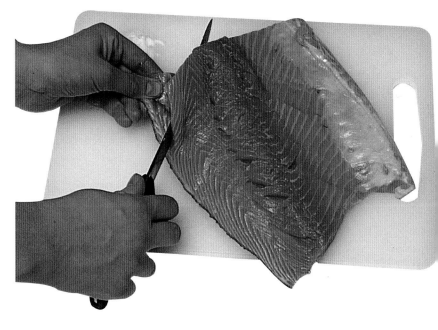

2 To remove the skin from the salmon, sprinkle the salt over the chopping board to prevent the fish slipping, then use a very sharp fish filleting knife.

3 Cut the fillet into strips, then place it in a non-metallic dish. Pour the teriyaki sauce over the fish and leave to marinate for 10–15 minutes.

4 To make the condiment, place the ginger in a bowl, mix in the food colouring, then stir in the mooli.

5 Lift the salmon from the teriyaki sauce and drain.

6 Heat the wok, then add the oil. When the oil is hot, add the salmon and stir-fry in batches for 3–4 minutes until the fish is cooked. Garnish with watercress and serve with the mooli and ginger condiment.

Fish Balls with Chinese Greens

These tasty fish balls are easy to make using a food processor. Here they are partnered with a selection of green vegetables – pak choi is available from oriental stores.

Serves 4

INGREDIENTS
FOR THE FISH BALLS
450 g/1 lb white fish fillets, skinned, boned and cubed
3 spring onions, chopped
1 back bacon rasher, rinded and chopped
15 ml/1 tbsp Chinese rice wine
30 ml/2 tbsp light soy sauce
1 egg white

FOR THE VEGETABLES
1 small head pak choi
5 ml/1 tsp cornflour
15 ml/1 tbsp light soy sauce
150 ml/¼ pint/⅔ cup fish stock
30 ml/2 tbsp groundnut oil
2 garlic cloves, sliced
2.5 cm/1 in piece fresh root ginger, cut into thin shreds
75 g/3 oz green beans
175 g/6 oz mange-touts
3 spring onions, sliced diagonally into 5–7.5cm/2–3 in lengths
salt and ground black pepper

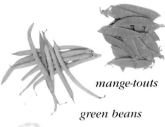

garlic *ginger*
bacon
spring onions
pak choi
light soy sauce
mange-touts
green beans *fish stock*
fish fillets
Chinese rice wine *groundnut oil*

1 Put the fish, spring onions, bacon, rice wine, soy sauce and egg white in a food processor. Process until smooth. With wetted hands, form the mixture into about 24 small balls.

2 Steam the fish balls in batches in a lightly greased bamboo steamer in a wok for 5–10 minutes until firm. Remove from the steamer and keep warm.

3 Meanwhile, trim the pak choi, removing any discoloured leaves or damaged stems, then tear into manageable pieces.

4 In a small bowl blend together the cornflour, soy sauce and stock. Set aside.

VARIATION

Replace the mange-touts and green beans with broccoli florets. Blanch them before stir-frying.

5 Heat a wok until hot, add the oil and swirl it around. Add the garlic and ginger and stir-fry for 1 minute. Add the beans and stir-fry for 2–3 minutes, then add the mange-touts, spring onions and pak choi. Stir-fry for 2–3 minutes.

6 Add the sauce to the wok and cook, stirring, until it has thickened and the vegetables are tender but crisp. Taste and adjust the seasoning, if necessary. Serve at once with the fish balls.

Lemon-grass-and-basil-scented Mussels

Thai flavourings of lemon grass and basil are used in this quick and easy dish.

Serves 4

INGREDIENTS
1.75 kg/4–4½ lb fresh mussels in the shell
2 lemon grass stalks
handful of small fresh basil leaves
5 cm/2 in piece fresh root ginger
2 shallots, finely chopped
150 ml/¼ pint/⅔ cup fish stock

lemon grass

mussels

fish stock

shallots

ginger

basil

1 Scrub the mussels under cold running water, scraping off any barnacles with a small sharp knife. Pull or cut off the hairy "beards". Discard any with damaged shells and any that remain open when sharply tapped.

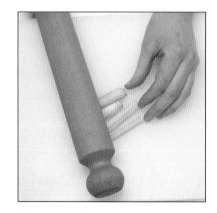

2 Cut each lemon grass stalk in half and bruise with a rolling pin.

3 Roughly chop half the basil leaves; reserve the remainder for the garnish.

4 Put the mussels, lemon grass, chopped basil, ginger, shallots and stock in a wok. Bring to the boil, cover and simmer for 5 minutes. Discard any mussels that remain closed. Scatter over the reserved basil and serve at once.

COOK'S TIP
Mussels are best bought fresh and eaten on the day of purchase. Any that remain closed after cooking should be thrown away.

Spicy Battered Fish

These crispy, spicy fritters are based on a dish from Baltistan, India.

Serves 4

INGREDIENTS
10 ml/2 tsp cumin seeds
10 ml/2 tsp coriander seeds
1–2 dried red chillies
30 ml/2 tbsp vegetable oil
175 g/6 oz/1½ cups gram flour
5 ml/1 tsp salt
10 ml/2 tsp garam masala
about 250 ml/8 fl oz/1 cup water
groundnut oil, for deep-frying
675 g/1½ lb fish fillets, such as
    cod, skinned, boned and cut
    into thick strips
mint sprigs and lime halves,
    to garnish

fish fillets

groundnut oil

gram flour

red chillies

vegetable oil

coriander

garam masala

1 Crush the cumin, coriander and chilli(es), using a pestle and mortar. Heat the vegetable oil in a karahi or wok and stir-fry the spices for 1–2 minutes.

2 Put the gram flour, salt, spice mixture and garam masala in a bowl. Gradually stir in enough water to make a thick batter. Cover and leave to rest for 30 minutes.

3 Half-fill a karahi or wok with groundnut oil and heat to 190°C/375°F. When the oil is ready, dip the fish, a few pieces at a time, into the batter, shaking off any excess.

4 Deep fry the fish in batches for 4–5 minutes until golden brown. Drain on kitchen paper. Serve immediately, garnished with mint sprigs and lime halves for squeezing over.

Red Snapper with Ginger and Spring Onions

This is a classic Chinese way of cooking fish. Pouring the oil slowly over the spring onions and ginger allows it to partially cook them, enhancing their flavour.

Serves 2-3

INGREDIENTS
1 red snapper, about
    675-900 g/1½-2 lb, cleaned and
    scaled with head left on
1 bunch spring onions, cut into
    thin shreds
2.5 cm/1 in piece fresh root
    ginger, cut into thin shreds
1.5 ml/¼ tsp salt
1.5 ml/¼ tsp caster sugar
45 ml/3 tbsp groundnut oil
5 ml/1 tsp sesame oil
30-45 ml/2-3 tbsp light soy sauce
spring onion brushes, to garnish

spring onions

ginger

groundnut oil

sesame oil

red snapper

caster sugar

light soy sauce

COOK'S TIP
If the fish is too big to fit inside the steamer, cut off the head and place it alongside the body - it can then be reassembled after it is cooked for serving.

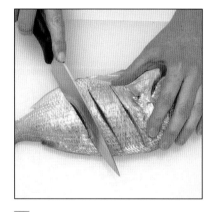

1 Rinse the fish, then pat dry with kitchen paper. Slash the flesh diagonally, three times on each side. Set the fish on a heatproof oval plate that will fit inside your bamboo steamer.

2 Tuck about one-third of the spring onions and ginger inside the body cavity. Place the plate inside the steamer, cover with its lid, then place in a wok.

3 Steam over a medium heat for 10–15 minutes until the fish flakes easily when tested with the tip of a knife.

4 Carefully remove the plate from the steamer. Sprinkle over the salt, sugar and remaining spring onions and ginger.

5 Heat the oils in a small pan until very hot, then slowly pour over the fish.

6 Drizzle over the soy sauce and serve at once, garnished with spring onion brushes.

FISH AND SEAFOOD DISHES

Stir-fried Squid with Black Bean Sauce

If you cannot buy fresh squid you will find small or baby frozen squid, ready skinned, boned and with heads removed, at your local Oriental supermarket.

Serves 4

INGREDIENTS
1 large or 2 medium-sized squid
1 red chilli
10 ml/2 tsp peanut oil
1 clove garlic, crushed
30 ml/2 tbsp black bean sauce
60 ml/4 tbsp water
fresh parsley sprigs, to garnish
steamed rice, to serve

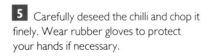
black bean sauce

squid

garlic

chillies

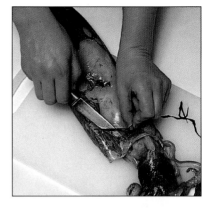

1 Carefully remove the skin from the squid and discard.

2 Cut off the head of each squid just below the eye, and discard.

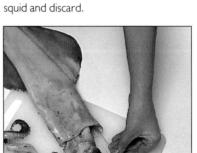

3 Remove the bone from the squid and discard.

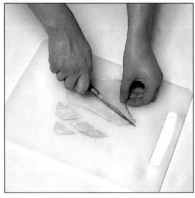

4 Cut the squid into bite-size pieces and score the flesh in a criss-cross pattern with a sharp knife.

5 Carefully deseed the chilli and chop it finely. Wear rubber gloves to protect your hands if necessary.

6 Heat the wok, then add the oil. When the oil is hot, add the garlic and cook until it starts to sizzle but does not colour. Stir in the squid and fry until the flesh starts to stiffen and turn white. Quickly stir in the black bean sauce, water and chilli. Continue stirring until the squid is cooked and tender (not more than a minute). Garnish with parsley sprigs and the tentacles and serve with steamed rice.

Green Seafood Curry

This curry is based on a Thai classic. The lovely green colour is imparted by the finely chopped chilli and fresh herbs added during the last few moments of cooking.

Serves 4

INGREDIENTS

225 g/8 oz small ready-prepared squid
225 g/8 oz raw tiger prawns
400 ml/14 fl oz/1¾ cups coconut milk
30 ml/2 tbsp green curry paste
2 fresh kaffir lime leaves, finely shredded
30 ml/2 tbsp Thai fish sauce (nam pla)
450 g/1 lb firm white fish fillets, skinned, boned and cut into chunks
2 fresh green chillies, seeded and finely chopped
30 ml/2 tbsp torn basil or coriander leaves
squeeze of lime juice
Thai jasmine rice, to serve

prawns

green chillies

squid

white fish

basil

coconut milk

green curry paste

kaffir lime leaves

1 Rinse the squid and pat dry with kitchen paper. Cut the bodies into rings and halve the tentacles, if necessary.

2 Heat a wok until hot, add the prawns and stir-fry without any oil for about 4 minutes until they turn pink.

3 Remove the prawns from the heat and when they are cool enough to handle, peel off the shells. Make a slit along the back of each one and remove the dark black vein.

4 Pour the coconut milk into the wok, then bring to the boil, stirring. Add the curry paste, shredded lime leaves and fish sauce. Reduce the heat to a simmer and cook for about 10 minutes, enough for the flavours to develop.

5 Add the squid, prawns and white fish and cook for about 2 minutes until the seafood is tender. Take care not to overcook the squid as it will become tough very quickly.

6 Just before serving, stir in the chillies and basil or coriander. Taste and adjust the flavour with a squeeze of lime juice. Serve with Thai jasmine rice.

Spiced Prawns with Coconut

This spicy dish is based on *Sambal Goreng Udang*, which is Indonesian in origin. It is best served with plain boiled rice.

Serves 3-4

INGREDIENTS

2-3 fresh red chillies, seeded and chopped
3 shallots, chopped
1 lemon grass stalk, chopped
2 garlic cloves, chopped
thin sliver of dried shrimp paste
2.5 ml/½ tsp ground galangal
5 ml/1 tsp ground turmeric
5 ml/1 tsp ground coriander
15 ml/1 tbsp groundnut oil
250 ml/8 fl oz/1 cup water
2 fresh kaffir lime leaves
5 ml/1 tsp light brown soft sugar
2 tomatoes, peeled, seeded and chopped
250 ml/8 fl oz/1 cup coconut milk
675 g/1½ lb large raw prawns, peeled and deveined
squeeze of lemon juice
salt, to taste
shredded spring onions and flaked coconut, to garnish

1 In a mortar pound the chillies, shallots, lemon grass, garlic, shrimp paste, galangal, turmeric and coriander with a pestle until it forms a paste.

prawns
turmeric
red chillies
garlic
lemon grass
dried shrimp paste
coriander
galangal
groundnut oil
coconut milk
sugar
tomatoes
shallots
kaffir lime leaves

COOK'S TIP

Dried shrimp paste, much used in South-east Asia, is available from oriental stores.

2 Heat a wok until hot, add the oil and swirl it around. Add the spiced paste and stir-fry for about 2 minutes. Pour in the water and add the kaffir lime leaves, sugar and tomatoes. Simmer for 8–10 minutes until most of the liquid has evaporated.

3 Add the coconut milk and prawns and cook gently, stirring, for about 4 minutes until the prawns are pink. Taste and adjust the seasoning with salt and a squeeze of lemon juice. Serve at once, garnished with shredded spring onions and toasted flaked coconut.

Sea Bass with Chinese Chives

Chinese chives are widely available in Oriental supermarkets but if you are unable to buy them, use half a large Spanish onion, finely sliced, instead.

Serves 4

INGREDIENTS
4 sea bass fillets, about 450 g/1 lb in all
5 ml/1 tsp cornflour
45 ml/3 tbsp vegetable oil
175 g/6 oz Chinese chives
15 ml/1 tbsp rice wine
5 ml/1 tsp caster sugar
salt and freshly ground pepper
Chinese chives with flowerheads,
    to garnish

sea bass

cornflour

rice wine

Chinese chives

1 Remove the scales from the bass by scraping the fillets with the back of a knife, working from tail end to head end.

2 Cut the fillets into large chunks and dust them lightly with cornflour, salt and pepper.

3 Heat the wok, then add 30 ml/2 tbsp of the oil. When the oil is hot, toss the chunks of fish in the wok briefly to seal, then set aside. Wipe out the wok with kitchen towels.

4 Cut the Chinese chives into 5 cm/2 in lengths and discard the flowers. Heat the wok and add the remaining oil, then stir-fry the Chinese chives for 30 seconds. Add the fish and rice wine, then bring to the boil and stir in the sugar. Serve hot, garnished with some flowering Chinese chives, and with a side dish of crisp mixed lettuce salad.

Fragrant Swordfish with Ginger and Lemon Grass

Swordfish is a meaty fish which cooks well in a wok if it has been marinated as a steak rather than in strips. If you cannot get swordfish, use tuna.

Serves 4

INGREDIENTS
1 kaffir lime leaf
45 ml/3 tbsp rock salt
75 ml/5 tbsp brown sugar
4 swordfish steaks, about
   225 g/8 oz each
1 stalk lemon grass, sliced
2.5 cm/1 in piece root ginger, cut into
   matchsticks
1 lime
15 ml/1 tbsp grapeseed oil
1 large ripe avocado, peeled and
   stoned
salt and freshly ground black pepper

avocado

ginger

lemon grass

lime

lime leaf

swordfish steak

1 Bruise the lime leaf by crushing slightly, to release the flavour.

2 To make the marinade, process the rock salt, brown sugar and lime leaf together in a food processor until thoroughly blended.

3 Place the swordfish steaks in a bowl. Sprinkle the marinade over them and add the lemon grass and ginger. Leave for 3–4 hours to marinate.

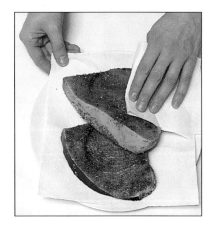

4 Rinse off the marinade and pat dry with kitchen towels.

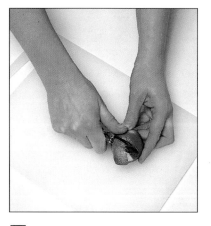

5 Peel the lime. Remove any excess pith from the peel, then cut into very thin strips.

6 Heat the wok, then add the oil. When the oil is hot, add the lime rind and then the steaks, and stir-fry for 3–4 minutes. Add the juice of the lime. Remove from the heat, slice the avocado and add to the fish. Season and serve.

Squid with Peppers in a Black Bean Sauce

Salted black beans add a traditionally Chinese flavour to this tasty stir-fry.

Serves 4

INGREDIENTS

30 ml/2 tbsp salted black beans
30 ml/2 tbsp medium-dry sherry
15 ml/1 tbsp light soy sauce
5 ml/1 tsp cornflour
2.5 ml/½ tsp sugar
30 ml/2 tbsp water
45 ml/3 tbsp groundnut oil
450 g/1 lb ready-prepared squid, scored and cut into thick strips
5 ml/1 tsp finely chopped fresh root ginger
1 garlic clove, finely chopped
1 fresh green chilli, seeded and sliced
6–8 spring onions, cut diagonally into 2.5 cm/1 in lengths
½ red and ½ green pepper, cored seeded and cut into 2.5 cm/1 in diamonds
75g/3 oz shiitake mushrooms, thickly sliced

spring onions

shiitake mushrooms

medium-dry sherry

light soy sauce

ginger

red pepper

squid

salted black beans   *green pepper*   *green chilli*

1 Rinse and finely chop the black beans. Place them in a bowl with the sherry, soy sauce, cornflour, sugar and water; mix well.

2 Heat a wok until hot, add the oil and swirl it around. When the oil is very hot, add the squid and stir-fry for 1–1½ minutes until opaque and curled at the edges. Remove with a slotted spoon and set aside.

3 Add the ginger, garlic and chilli to the wok and stir-fry for a few seconds. Add the spring onions, peppers and mushrooms, then stir-fry for 2 minutes.

4 Return the squid to the wok with the sauce. Cook, stirring, for about 1 minute until thickened. Serve at once.

Spicy Crab and Coconut

This spicy dish is delicious served with plain warm Naan bread.

Serves 4

INGREDIENTS

40 g/1½ oz dried unsweetened
 coconut flakes
2 cloves garlic
5 cm/2 in piece root ginger,
 peeled and grated
2.5 ml/½ tsp cumin seeds
1 small stick cinnamon
2.5 ml/½ tsp ground turmeric
2 dried red chillies
15 ml/1 tbsp coriander seeds
2.5 ml/½ tsp poppy seeds
15 ml/1 tbsp vegetable oil
1 medium onion, sliced
1 small green pepper, cut into strips
16 crab claws
fresh coriander sprigs, crushed,
to garnish
150 ml/¼ pint/⅔ cup natural low-fat
 yogurt, to serve

pepper

cumin seeds

cinnamon

*crab
claw*

1 Place the dried coconut, garlic, ginger, cumin seeds, cinnamon, turmeric, red chillies, coriander and poppy seeds into a food processor and process until well blended.

2 Heat the oil in the wok and fry the onion until soft, but not coloured.

3 Stir in the green pepper and stir-fry for 1 minute.

4 Remove the vegetables with a slotted spoon and heat the wok. Add the crab claws, stir-fry for 2 minutes, then briefly return all the spiced vegetables to the wok. Garnish with fresh coriander sprigs and serve with the cooling yogurt.

Sweet-and-sour Fish

The combination of sweet and sour is a popular one in many cuisines. The sauce can be made up to two days in advance.

COOK'S TIP
When buying the fish for this dish, select fillets which are 2 cm/¾ in or more thick.

Serves 3-4

INGREDIENTS
450 g/1 lb white fish fillets, skinned, boned and cubed
2.5 ml/½ tsp Chinese five-spice powder
5 ml/1 tsp light soy sauce
1 egg, lightly beaten
30-45 ml/2-3 tbsp cornflour
groundnut oil, for deep-frying

FOR THE SAUCE
10 ml/2 tsp cornflour
60 ml/4 tbsp water
60 ml/4 tbsp pineapple juice
45 ml/3 tbsp Chinese rice vinegar
45 ml/3 tbsp caster sugar
10 ml/2 tsp light soy sauce
30 ml/2 tbsp tomato ketchup
10 ml/2 tsp Chinese rice wine or medium-dry sherry
45 ml/3 tbsp groundnut oil
1 garlic clove, crushed
15 ml/1 tbsp chopped fresh root ginger
6 spring onions, sliced diagonally into 5 cm/2 in lengths
1 green pepper, seeded and cut into 2 cm/¾ in pieces
115 g/4 oz fresh pineapple, cut into 2cm/¾ in pieces
salt and ground black pepper

light soy sauce

white fish

spring onion

garlic

cornflour

egg

green pepper

Chinese rice wine

ginger

Chinese five-spice powder

pineapple

tomato ketchup

1 Put the fish in a bowl. Sprinkle over the five-spice powder and soy sauce, then toss gently. Cover and leave to marinate for about 30 minutes. Dip the fish in the egg, then in the cornflour, shaking off any excess.

2 Half-fill a wok with oil and heat to 190°C/375°F. Deep fry the fish in batches for about 2 minutes until golden. Drain and keep warm. Carefully pour off all the oil from the wok and wipe clean.

3 To make the sauce, blend together in a bowl the cornflour, water, pineapple juice, rice vinegar, sugar, soy sauce, ketchup and rice wine or sherry. Mix well, then set aside.

4 Heat the wok until hot, add 30 ml/ 2 tbsp of the oil and swirl it around. Add the garlic and ginger and stir-fry for a few seconds. Add the spring onions and green pepper and stir-fry over a medium heat for 2 minutes. Add the pineapple.

5 Pour in the sauce and cook, stirring until thickened. Stir in the remaining 15 ml/1 tbsp oil and add seasoning to taste. Pour the sauce over the fish and serve at once.

Thai Fish Stir-fry

This is a substantial dish: it is best served with chunks of fresh crusty white bread, for mopping up all the delicious, spicy juices.

Serves 4

INGREDIENTS
675 g/1½ lb mixed seafood (for example, red snapper, cod, raw prawn tails) filleted and skinned
300 ml/½ pint/1¼ cups coconut milk
15 ml/1 tbsp vegetable oil
salt and freshly ground black pepper

FOR THE SAUCE
2 large red chillies
1 onion, roughly chopped
5 cm/2 in piece root ginger, peeled and sliced
5 cm/2 in piece lemon grass, outer leaf discarded, roughly sliced
5 cm/2 in piece galingale, peeled and sliced
6 blanched almonds, chopped
2.5 ml/½ tsp turmeric
2.5 ml/½ tsp salt

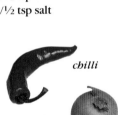
chilli
onion

ginger
prawn

1 Cut the filleted fish into large chunks. Peel the prawns, keeping their tails intact.

2 Carefully remove the seeds from the chillies and chop roughly, wearing rubber gloves to protect your hands if necessary. Then, make the sauce by putting the chillies and the other sauce ingredients in the food processor with 45 ml/3 tbsp of the coconut milk. Blend until smooth.

3 Heat the wok, then add the oil. When the oil is hot, stir-fry the seafood for 2–3 minutes, then remove.

4 Add the sauce and the remaining coconut milk to the wok, then return the seafood. Bring to the boil, season well and serve with crusty bread.

Spiced Scallops in their Shells

Scallops are excellent steamed. When served with this spicy sauce, they make a delicious yet simple starter. Each person spoons sauce on to the scallops before eating them.

Serves 4

INGREDIENTS
8 scallops, shelled (ask the
 fishmonger to reserve the
 cupped side of 4 shells)
2 slices fresh root ginger,
 shredded
½ garlic clove, shredded
2 spring onions, green parts only,
 shredded
salt and pepper

FOR THE SAUCE
1 garlic clove, crushed
15 ml/1 tbsp grated fresh
 root ginger
2 spring onions, white parts
 only, chopped
1–2 fresh green chillies, seeded
 and finely chopped
15 ml/1 tbsp light soy sauce
15 ml/1 tbsp dark soy sauce
10 ml/2 tsp sesame oil

scallops

ginger

spring onions

light soy sauce

garlic

green chilli

dark soy sauce   sesame oil

I Remove the dark beard-like fringe and tough muscle from the scallops.

2 Place 2 scallops in each shell. Season lightly with salt and pepper, then scatter the ginger, garlic and spring onions on top. Place the shells in a bamboo steamer and steam for about 6 minutes until the scallops look opaque (you may have to do this in batches).

3 Meanwhile, mix together all the sauce ingredients and pour into a small serving bowl.

4 Carefully remove each shell from the steamer, taking care not to spill the juices, and arrange them on a serving plate with the sauce bowl in the centre. Serve at once.

Pan-fried Red Mullet with Lemon

This spectacularly attractive and delicious dish is well worth the time it takes to prepare.

Serves 4

INGREDIENTS
1 large bulb fennel
1 lemon
12 red mullet fillets, skin left intact
45 ml/3 tbsp fresh marjoram, chopped
45 ml/3 tbsp olive oil
225 g/8 oz lamb's lettuce
salt and freshly ground black pepper

FOR THE VINAIGRETTE
200 ml/7 fl oz/generous ¾ cup
    peanut oil
15 ml/1 tbsp white wine vinegar
15 ml/1 tbsp sherry vinegar
salt and freshly ground black pepper

FOR THE SAUCE
40 g/1½ oz black olives
15 g/½ oz/1 tbsp unsalted butter
25 g/1 oz/1 tbsp capers

fennel

red mullet

marjoram

lamb's lettuce

1 Trim the fennel bulb and cut it into fine matchsticks. Peel the lemon. Remove any excess pith from the peel, then cut it into fine strips. Blanch the rind and refresh it immediately in cold water. Drain.

2 Make the vinaigrette by placing all the ingredients in a small bowl and lightly whisking until well mixed.

3 Sprinkle the red mullet fillets with salt, pepper and marjoram.

4 Heat the wok and add the olive oil. When the oil is very hot, add the fennel and stir-fry for 1 minute, then drain and remove.

5 Reheat the wok and, when the oil is hot, stir-fry the red mullet fillets, cooking them skin-side down first for 2 minutes, then flipping them over for 1 further minute. Drain well on kitchen towels and wipe the wok clean with kitchen towels.

6 For the sauce, cut the olives into slivers. Heat the wok and add the butter. When the butter is hot, stir-fry the capers and olives for 1 minute. Toss the lamb's lettuce in the dressing. Arrange the fillets on a bed of lettuce, topped with the fennel and lemon, and serve with the olive and caper sauce.

Spiced Salmon Stir-fry

Marinating the salmon allows all the flavours to develop, and the lime tenderizes the fish beautifully, so it needs very little stir-frying – be careful not to overcook it.

Serves 4

INGREDIENTS
4 salmon steaks, about
 225 g/8 oz each
4 whole star anise
2 stalks lemon grass, sliced
juice of 3 limes
rind of 3 limes, finely grated
30 ml/2 tbsp clear honey
30 ml/2 tbsp grapeseed oil
salt and freshly ground black pepper
lime wedges, to garnish

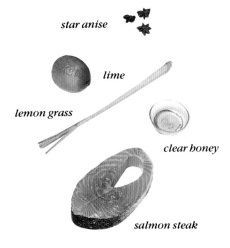

star anise

lime

lemon grass

clear honey

salmon steak

COOK'S TIP

Always dry off any marinade from meat, fish or vegetables to ensure that the hot oil does not splutter when you add them to the wok.

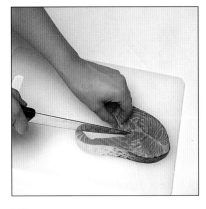

1 Remove the middle bone from each steak, using a very sharp filleting knife, to make two strips from each steak.

2 Remove the skin by inserting the knife at the thin end of each piece of salmon. Sprinkle 5 ml/1 tsp salt on the cutting board to prevent the fish slipping while removing the skin. Slice into pieces using diagonal cuts.

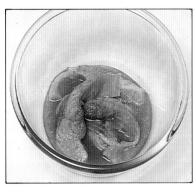

3 Coarsely crush the star anise in a pestle and mortar. Marinate the salmon in a non-metallic dish, with the star anise, lemon grass, lime juice and rind and honey. Season well with salt and pepper, cover and chill overnight.

4 Carefully drain the salmon from the marinade, pat dry on kitchen towels, and reserve the marinade.

5 Heat the wok, then add the oil. When the oil is hot, add the salmon and stir-fry, stirring constantly until cooked. Increase the heat, pour over the marinade and bring to the boil. Garnish with lime wedges and serve.

Oriental Scallops with Ginger Relish

Buy scallops in their shells to be absolutely sure of their freshness; your fishmonger will open them for you if you find this difficult. Remember to ask for the shells, which make excellent serving dishes.

Serves 4

INGREDIENTS
8 king or queen scallops
4 whole star anise
25 g/1 oz/2 tbsp unsalted butter
salt and freshly ground white pepper
fresh chervil sprigs and whole star
   anise, to garnish

FOR THE RELISH
½ cucumber, peeled
salt, for sprinkling
5 cm/2 in piece root ginger, peeled
10 ml/2 tsp caster sugar
45 ml/3 tbsp rice wine vinegar
10 ml/2 tsp ginger juice, strained from
   a jar of stem ginger
sesame seeds, for sprinkling

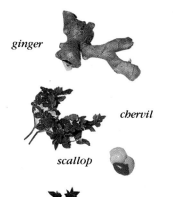

ginger

chervil

scallop

star anise

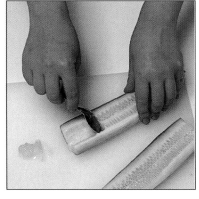

1 To make the relish, halve the cucumber lengthways and scoop out the seeds with a teaspoon.

2 Cut the cucumber into 2.5 cm/1 in pieces, place in a colander and sprinkle liberally with salt. Set aside for 30 minutes.

3 To prepare the scallops, cut each into 2–3 slices. Coarsely grind the star anise in a pestle and mortar.

4 Place the scallop slices with the corals in a bowl and marinate with the star anise and seasoning for about 1 hour.

5 Rinse the cucumber under cold water and pat dry on kitchen towels. Cut the ginger into thin julienne strips and mix with the remaining relish ingredients. Cover and chill until needed.

6 Heat the wok and add the butter. When the butter is hot, add the scallop slices and stir-fry for 2–3 minutes. Garnish with sprigs of chervil and whole star anise, and serve with the cucumber relish, sprinkled with sesame seeds.

Chicken Liver Stir-fry

The final sprinkling of lemon, parsley and garlic gives this dish a delightful fresh flavour and wonderful aroma.

Serves 4

INGREDIENTS

500 g/1¼ lb chicken livers
75 g/3 oz/6 tbsp butter
175 g/6 oz field mushrooms
50 g/2 oz chanterelle mushrooms
3 cloves garlic, finely chopped
2 shallots, finely chopped
150 ml/¼ pint/⅔ cup medium sherry
3 fresh rosemary sprigs
30 ml/2 tbsp fresh parsley, chopped
rind of 1 lemon, grated
salt and freshly ground pepper
fresh rosemary sprigs, to garnish
4 thick slices of white toast, to serve

1 Clean and trim the chicken livers to remove any gristle or muscle.

2 Season the livers generously with salt and freshly ground black pepper, tossing well to coat thoroughly.

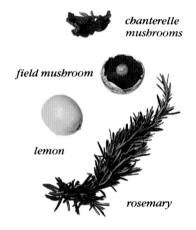

chanterelle mushrooms

field mushroom

lemon

rosemary

3 Heat the wok and add 15 g/½ oz/1 tbsp of the butter. When melted, add the livers in batches (melting more butter where necessary but reserving 25 g/1 oz/2 tbsp for the vegetables) and flash-fry until golden brown. Drain with a slotted spoon and transfer to a plate, then place in a low oven to keep warm.

4 Cut the field mushrooms into thick slices and, depending on the size of the chanterelles, cut in half.

5 Heat the wok and add the remaining butter. When melted, stir in two-thirds of the chopped garlic and the shallots and stir-fry for 1 minute until golden brown. Stir in the mushrooms and continue to cook for a further 2 minutes.

6 Add the sherry, bring to the boil and simmer for 2–3 minutes until syrupy. Add the rosemary, salt and pepper and return livers to the pan. Stir-fry for 1 minute. Garnish with extra sprigs of rosemary, and serve sprinkled with a mixture of lemon, parsley and the remaining chopped garlic, with slices of toast.

Beef Rendang

In this curry from Indonesia, the meat is simmered in a mixture of coconut milk and spices until the liquid has almost disappeared, leaving dark, intensely flavoured meat.

Serves 4

INGREDIENTS
4 dried red chillies
7.5 cm/3 in piece galangal
6 shallots, chopped
1 small red pepper, seeded and chopped
4 garlic cloves, chopped
10 ml/2 tsp ground cinnamon
10 ml/2 tsp ground coriander
5 ml/1 tsp ground turmeric
5 ml/1 tsp ground cloves
15 ml/1 tbsp groundnut oil
1.5 litres/2½ pints/6¼ cups coconut milk
2 bay leaves
2 lemon grass stalks, bruised
3 fresh kaffir lime leaves
1 kg/2¼ lb stewing or braising steak, trimmed and cut into 5 cm/2 in cubes
5 ml/1 tsp salt
shredded kaffir lime leaves and red chilli flowers, to garnish
plain boiled rice, to serve

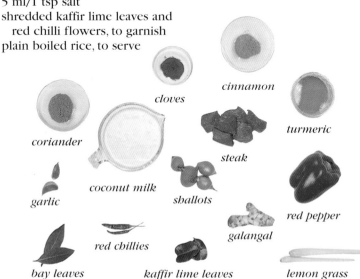

cloves

cinnamon

coriander

turmeric

steak

coconut milk

shallots

garlic

red pepper

red chillies

galangal

bay leaves

kaffir lime leaves

lemon grass

COOK'S TIP
This curry tastes even better if made the day before and kept covered in the fridge. Reheat it on top of the stove until piping hot before serving.

1 Crumble or break the chillies into a bowl. Add 60 ml/4 tbsp water and leave to soak for 30 minutes.

2 Peel and roughly chop the galangal.

3 Put the soaked chillies and their liquid, the galangal, the chopped shallots, pepper, garlic and remaining spices into a blender or food processor and blend until smooth.

4 Heat a wok until hot, add the oil and swirl it around. Add the spice paste and stir-fry for about 2 minutes. Pour in the coconut milk and add the bay leaves, lemon grass and kaffir lime leaves. Bring to the boil, stirring constantly.

5 Add the meat and salt. Reduce the heat and simmer, uncovered for 2–2½ hours, stirring occasionally, until most of the liquid has evaporated. Towards the end of cooking, stir the meat more frequently to prevent it sticking. Taste and season if necessary. Garnish with shredded kaffir lime leaves and red chilli flowers. Serve with plain boiled rice.

Paper-thin Lamb with Spring Onions

Spring onions lend a delicious flavour to the lamb in this simple supper dish.

Serves 3-4

INGREDIENTS
450 g/1 lb lamb fillet
30 ml/2 tbsp Chinese rice wine
10 ml/2 tsp light soy sauce
2.5 ml/½ tsp roasted and ground
   Szechuan peppercorns
2.5 ml/½ tsp salt
2.5 m/½ tsp dark brown soft sugar
20 ml/4 tsp dark soy sauce
15 ml/1 tbsp sesame oil
30 ml/2 tbsp groundnut oil
2 garlic cloves, thinly sliced
2 bunches spring onions, cut
   into 7.5 cm/3 in lengths,
   then shredded
30 ml/2 tbsp chopped
   fresh coriander

spring onions

lamb

dark soy sauce

sesame oil

salt

Chinese rice wine

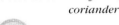

coriander

garlic

groundnut oil

1 Wrap the lamb and place in the freezer for about 1 hour until just frozen. Cut the meat across the grain into paper-thin slices. Put the lamb slices in a bowl, add 10 ml/2 tsp of the rice wine, the light soy sauce and ground Szechuan peppercorns. Mix well and leave to marinate for 15–30 minutes.

2 Make the sauce: in a bowl mix together the remaining rice wine, the salt, brown sugar, dark soy sauce and 10ml/2 tsp of the sesame oil. Set aside.

3 Heat a wok until hot, add the oil and swirl it around. Add the garlic and let it sizzle for a few seconds, then add the lamb. Stir-fry for about 1 minute until the lamb is no longer pink. Pour in the sauce and stir briefly.

4 Add the spring onions and coriander and stir-fry for 15–20 seconds until the spring onions just wilt. The finished dish should be slightly dry in appearance. Serve at once, sprinkled with the remaining sesame oil.

Veal Escalopes with Artichokes

Artichokes are very hard to prepare fresh, so use canned artichoke hearts, instead – they have an excellent flavour and are simple to use.

Serves 4

INGREDIENTS
450 g/1 lb veal escalopes
1 shallot
115 g/4 oz smoked bacon,
  finely chopped
1 × 400 g/14 oz can of artichoke
  hearts in brine, drained and
  quartered
150 ml/¼ pint/⅔ cup veal stock
3 fresh rosemary sprigs
60 ml/4 tbsp double cream
salt and freshly ground black pepper
fresh rosemary sprigs, to garnish

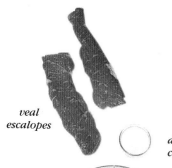

veal escalopes

double cream

artichoke hearts

1 Cut the veal into thin slices.

2 Using a sharp knife, cut the shallot into thin slices.

3 Heat the wok, then add the bacon. Stir-fry for 2 minutes. When the fat is released, add the veal and shallot and stir-fry for 3–4 minutes.

4 Add the artichokes and stir-fry for 1 minute. Stir in the stock and rosemary and simmer for 2 minutes. Stir in the double cream, season with salt and pepper and serve garnished with sprigs of fresh rosemary.

Indonesian-style Satay Chicken

Use boneless chicken thighs to give a good flavour to these satays.

Serves 4

INGREDIENTS
50 g/2 oz/½ cup raw peanuts
45 ml/3 tbsp vegetable oil
1 small onion, finely chopped
2.5 cm/1 in piece root ginger, peeled
   and finely chopped
1 clove garlic, crushed
675 g/1½ lb chicken thighs, skinned
   and cut into cubes
90 g/3½ oz creamed coconut,
   roughly chopped
15 ml/1 tbsp chilli sauce
60 ml/4 tbsp crunchy peanut butter
5 ml/1 tsp soft dark brown sugar
150 ml/¼ pint/⅔ cup milk
1.2 ml/¼ tsp salt

COOK'S TIP
Soak bamboo skewers in cold water for at least 2 hours, or preferably overnight, so they do not char when keeping the threaded chicken warm in the oven.

1 Shell and rub the skins from the peanuts, then soak them in enough water to cover, for 1 minute. Drain the nuts and cut them into slivers.

2 Heat the wok and add 5 ml/1 tsp oil. When the oil is hot, stir-fry the peanuts for 1 minute until crisp and golden. Remove with a slotted spoon and drain on kitchen towels.

3 Add the remaining oil to the hot wok. When the oil is hot, add the onion, ginger and garlic and stir-fry for 2–3 minutes until softened but not browned. Remove with a slotted spoon and drain on kitchen towels.

creamed coconut

peanuts

chilli sauce

peanut butter

4 Add the chicken pieces and stir-fry for 3–4 minutes until crisp and golden on all sides. Thread on to pre-soaked bamboo skewers and keep warm.

5 Add the creamed coconut to the hot wok in small pieces and stir-fry until melted. Add the chilli sauce, peanut butter and cooked ginger and garlic, and simmer for 2 minutes. Stir in the sugar, milk and salt, and simmer for a further 3 minutes. Serve the skewered chicken hot, with a dish of the hot dipping sauce sprinkled with the roasted peanuts.

Chilli Beef with Basil

This is a dish for chilli lovers! It is very easy to prepare and cook.

Serves 2

INGREDIENTS

about 90 ml/6 tbsp groundnut oil
16–20 large fresh basil leaves
275 g/10 oz rump steak
30 ml/2 tbsp Thai fish sauce
  (*nam pla*)
5 ml/1 tsp dark brown soft sugar
1–2 fresh red chillies, sliced
  into rings
3 garlic cloves, chopped
5 ml/1 tsp chopped fresh
  root ginger
1 shallot, thinly sliced
30 ml/2 tbsp finely chopped fresh
  basil leaves
squeeze of lemon juice
salt and ground black pepper
Thai jasmine rice, to serve

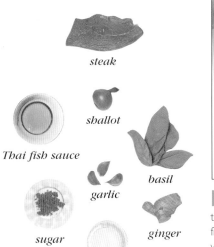

steak

shallot

Thai fish sauce

basil

garlic

sugar

ginger

groundnut oil

red chilli

1 Heat the oil in a wok and, when hot, add the basil leaves and fry for about 1 minute until crisp and golden. Drain on kitchen paper. Remove the wok from the heat and pour off all but 30 ml/2 tbsp of the oil.

2 Cut the steak across the grain into thin strips. In a bowl mix together the fish sauce and sugar. Add the beef, mix well, then leave to marinate for about 30 minutes.

3 Reheat the oil until hot, add the chilli(es), garlic, ginger and shallot and stir-fry for 30 seconds. Add the beef and chopped basil, then stir-fry for about 3 minutes. Flavour with lemon juice and add seasoning to taste.

4 Transfer to a serving plate, scatter over the basil leaves and serve immediately with Thai jasmine rice.

Lemon Grass Pork

Chillies and lemon grass flavour this simple stir-fry, while peanuts add crunch.

Serves 4

INGREDIENTS

675 g/1½ lb boneless loin of pork
2 lemon grass stalks,
    finely chopped
4 spring onions, thinly sliced
5 ml/1 tsp salt
12 black peppercorns,
    coarsely crushed
30 ml/2 tbsp groundnut oil
2 garlic cloves, chopped
2 fresh red chillies, seeded
    and chopped
5 ml/1 tsp light brown soft sugar
30 ml/2 tbsp Thai fish sauce
    (nam pla), or to taste
25 g/1 oz/¼ cup roasted
    unsalted peanuts, chopped
salt and ground black pepper
rice noodles, to serve
roughly torn coriander leaves,
    to garnish

spring onions

red chillies

peanuts   pork

sugar   coriander

lemon grass

Thai fish sauce

garlic

groundnut oil

1 Trim any excess fat from the pork. Cut the meat across into 5 mm/¼ in thick slices, then cut each slice into 5 mm/¼ in strips. Put the pork into a bowl with the lemon grass, spring onions, salt and crushed peppercorns; mix well. Cover and leave to marinate for 30 minutes.

2 Heat a wok until hot, add the oil and swirl it around. Add the pork mixture and stir-fry for 3 minutes.

3 Add the garlic and chillies and stir-fry for a further 5–8 minutes over a medium heat until the pork no longer looks pink.

4 Add the sugar, fish sauce and peanuts, and toss to mix. Taste and adjust the seasoning, if necessary. Serve at once on a bed of rice noodles, garnished with roughly torn coriander leaves.

Glazed Chicken with Cashew Nuts

Hoisin sauce lends a sweet yet slightly hot note to this chicken dish, while cashew nuts add a pleasing contrast of texture.

VARIATION
Use blanched almonds instead of cashew nuts if you prefer.

Serves 4

INGREDIENTS
75 g/3 oz/¾ cup cashew nuts
1 red pepper
450 g/1 lb skinless and boneless
    chicken breasts
45 ml/3 tbsp groundnut oil
4 garlic cloves, finely chopped
30 ml/2 tbsp Chinese rice wine
    or medium-dry sherry
45 ml/3 tbsp hoisin sauce
10 ml/2 tsp sesame oil
5–6 spring onions, green parts
    only, cut into
    2.5 cm/1 in lengths

chicken

spring onion

red pepper

cashew nuts

Chinese rice wine

garlic

groundnut oil

hoisin sauce

sesame oil

1 Heat a wok until hot, add the cashew nuts and stir-fry over a low to medium heat for 1–2 minutes until golden brown. Remove and set aside.

2 Halve the pepper and remove the seeds. Slice the pepper and chicken into finger-length strips.

3 Heat the wok again until hot, add the oil and swirl it around. Add the garlic and let it sizzle in the oil for a few seconds. Add the pepper and chicken and stir-fry for 2 minutes.

4 Add the rice wine or sherry and hoisin sauce. Continue to stir-fry until the chicken is tender and all the ingredients are evenly glazed.

5 Stir in the sesame oil, toasted cashew nuts and spring onion tips. Serve immediately with rice or noodles.

Spiced Lamb with Spinach

This recipe is based on *Sag Gosht* – meat cooked with spinach. The whole spices in this dish are not meant to be eaten.

Serves 3-4

INGREDIENTS
45 ml/3 tbsp vegetable oil
500 g/1¼ lb lean boneless lamb,
    cut into 2.5 cm/1 in cubes
1 onion, chopped
3 garlic cloves, finely chopped
1 cm/½ in piece fresh root
    ginger, finely chopped
6 black peppercorns
4 whole cloves
1 bay leaf
3 green cardamom pods, crushed
5 ml/1 tsp ground cumin
5 ml/1 tsp ground coriander
generous pinch of
    cayenne pepper
150 ml/¼ pint/⅔ cup water
2 tomatoes, peeled, seeded
    and chopped
5 ml/1 tsp salt
400 g/14 oz fresh spinach,
    trimmed, washed and
    finely chopped
5 ml/1 tsp garam masala
crisp-fried onions and fresh
    coriander sprigs, to garnish
naan bread or spiced basmati
    rice, to serve

1 Heat a karahi or wok until hot. Add 30 ml/2 tbsp of the oil and swirl it around. When hot, stir-fry the lamb in batches until evenly browned. Remove the lamb and set aside. Add the remaining oil, onion, garlic and ginger and stir-fry for 2–3 minutes.

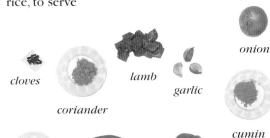

cloves

coriander

lamb

garlic

bay leaf

garam masala

spinach

ginger

cumin

onion

cardamom pods

cayenne pepper

tomatoes

2 Add the peppercorns, cloves, bay leaf, cardamom pods, cumin, coriander and cayenne pepper. Stir-fry for 30–45 seconds. Return the lamb and add the water, tomatoes and salt and bring to the boil. Simmer, covered, over a very low heat for about 1 hour, stirring occasionally until the meat is tender.

3 Increase the heat, then gradually add the spinach to the lamb, stirring to mix. Keep stirring and cooking until the spinach wilts completely and most, but not all of the liquid has evaporated and you are left with a thick green sauce. Stir in the garam masala. Garnish with crisp-fried onions and coriander sprigs. Serve with naan bread or spiced basmati rice.

Duck and Ginger Chop Suey

Chicken can also be used in this recipe, but duck gives a richer contrast of flavours.

Serves 4

INGREDIENTS
2 duck breasts, about 175 g/6 oz each
45 ml/3 tbsp sunflower oil
1 × size 4 egg, lightly beaten
1 clove garlic
175 g/6 oz beansprouts
2 slices root ginger, cut into
    matchsticks
10 ml/2 tsp oyster sauce
2 spring onions, cut into matchsticks
salt and freshly ground pepper

FOR THE MARINADE
15 ml/1 tbsp clear honey
10 ml/2 tsp rice wine
10 ml/2 tsp light soy sauce
10 ml/2 tsp dark soy sauce

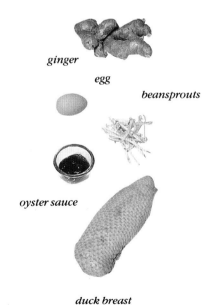

ginger

egg

beansprouts

oyster sauce

duck breast

1 Remove the fat from the duck, cut the breasts into thin strips and place in a bowl. Mix the marinade ingredients together, pour over the duck, cover, chill and marinate overnight.

2 Next day, make the egg omelette. Heat a small frying pan and add 15 ml/ 1 tbsp of the oil. When the oil is hot, pour in the egg and swirl around to make an omelette. Once cooked, leave it to cool and cut into strips. Drain the duck and discard the marinade.

3 Bruise the garlic with the flat blade of a knife. Heat the wok, then add 10 ml/ 2 tsp oil. When the oil is hot, add the garlic and fry for 30 seconds, pressing it to release the flavour. Discard. Add the beansprouts with seasoning and stir-fry for 30 seconds. Transfer to a heated dish, draining off any liquid.

4 Heat the wok and add the remaining oil. When the oil is hot, stir-fry the duck for 3 minutes until cooked. Add the ginger and oyster sauce and stir-fry for a further 2 minutes. Add the beansprouts, egg strips and spring onions, stir-fry briefly and serve.

Balti Chicken Tikka Masala

This recipe is based on *Makkhani Murghi*, a popular Balti dish. Serve with warm naan bread or fluffy basmati rice.

Serves 4

INGREDIENTS

FOR THE MARINATED CHICKEN
4 part-boned chicken breasts, skinned
150 ml/¼ pint/⅔ cup natural yogurt
2.5 cm/1 in piece fresh root ginger, grated
2 garlic cloves, crushed
5 ml/1 tsp chilli powder
15 ml/1 tbsp ground coriander
30 ml/2 tbsp vegetable oil
30 ml/2 tbsp lime juice
few drops each of yellow and red liquid food colouring, mixed to a bright orange shade

FOR THE MASALA
75 g/3 oz unsalted butter
15 ml/1 tbsp vegetable oil
1 onion, chopped
450 g/1 lb tomatoes, peeled, seeded and chopped
5 ml/1 tsp salt
1 fresh green chilli, seeded and finely chopped
5 ml/1 tsp garam masala
1.5 ml/¼ tsp cayenne pepper
120 ml/4 fl oz/½ cup double cream
45 ml/3 tbsp natural yogurt
30 ml/2 tbsp roughly torn fresh coriander leaves
5 ml/1 tsp dry-roasted cumin seeds

chilli powder
chicken
coriander
tomatoes
double cream
butter
cayenne pepper
ginger
vegetable oil
green chilli
onion
food colouring
coriander
yogurt

1 Cut each chicken breast into three or four pieces, then slash the meaty side of each piece. Put the chicken into a shallow dish. In a bowl, mix together the yogurt, ginger, garlic, chilli powder, ground coriander, oil, lime juice and colouring. Pour over the chicken and toss to coat completely, making sure that the marinade goes into the slits in the chicken. Cover and leave in the fridge for 6–24 hours, turning occasionally.

COOK'S TIP
If you can, leave the chicken to marinate for as long as possible to allow plenty of time for it to absorb the flavourings.

2 Preheat the oven to 230°C/450°F/Gas 8. Lift the chicken pieces out of the marinade, shaking off any excess, and arrange in a shallow baking tin. Bake for 15–20 minutes until golden brown and cooked through.

3 Meanwhile, make the masala: heat the butter and oil in a karahi or wok, add the onion and fry for 5 minutes until softened. Add the tomatoes, salt, chilli, garam masala and cayenne pepper. Cook, covered, for about 10 minutes.

4 Stir in the cream and yogurt, then simmer over a low heat for 1–2 minutes, stirring constantly. Add the chicken pieces, then stir to coat in the sauce. Serve at once sprinkled with coriander leaves and roasted cumin seeds.

Spiced Honey Chicken Wings

Be prepared to get very sticky when you eat these wings, as the best way to enjoy them is by eating them with your fingers. Provide individual finger bowls for your guests.

Serves 4

INGREDIENTS
1 red chilli, finely chopped
5 ml/1 tsp chilli powder
5 ml/1 tsp ground ginger
rind of 1 lime, finely grated
12 chicken wings
60 ml/4 tbsp sunflower oil
15 ml/1 tbsp fresh coriander, chopped
30 ml/2 tbsp soy sauce
50 ml/3½ tbsp clear honey
lime rind and fresh coriander sprigs,
    to garnish

lime

coriander

honey

chicken wing

1 Mix the fresh chilli, chilli powder, ground ginger and lime rind together. Rub the mixture into the chicken skins and leave for at least 2 hours to allow the flavours to penetrate.

2 Heat the wok and add half of the oil. When the oil is hot, add half the wings and stir-fry for 10 minutes, turning regularly until crisp and golden. Drain on kitchen towels. Repeat with the remaining wings.

4 Stir in the soy sauce and honey, and stir-fry for 1 minute. Serve the chicken wings hot with the sauce drizzled over them, garnished with lime rind and coriander sprigs.

3 Add the coriander to the hot wok and stir-fry for 30 seconds, then return the wings to the wok and stir-fry for 1 minute.

Stir-fried Duck with Blueberries

Serve this conveniently quick dinner party dish with sprigs of fresh mint, which will give a wonderful fresh aroma as you bring the meal to the table.

Serves 4

INGREDIENTS

2 duck breasts, about 175 g/6 oz each
30 ml/2 tbsp sunflower oil
15 ml/1 tbsp red wine vinegar
5 ml/1 tsp sugar
5 ml/1 tsp red wine
5 ml/1 tsp *crème de cassis*
115 g/4 oz fresh blueberries
15 ml/1 tbsp fresh mint, chopped
salt and freshly ground black pepper
fresh mint sprigs, to garnish

duck

red wine vinegar
blueberries

red wine

mint

1 Cut the duck breasts into neat slices. Season well with salt and pepper.

2 Heat the wok, then add the oil. When the oil is hot, stir-fry the duck for 3 minutes.

3 Add the red wine vinegar, sugar, red wine and *crème de cassis*. Bubble for 3 minutes, to reduce to a thick syrup.

4 Stir in the blueberries, sprinkle over the mint and serve garnished with sprigs of fresh mint.

Warm Stir-fried Salad

Warm salads are becoming increasingly popular because they are delicious and nutritious. Arrange the salad leaves on four individual plates, so the hot stir-fry can be served quickly on to them, ensuring the lettuce remains crisp and the chicken warm.

Serves 4

INGREDIENTS

15 ml/1 tbsp fresh tarragon
2 boneless, skinless chicken breasts, about 225 g/8 oz each
5 cm/2 in piece root ginger, peeled and finely chopped
45 ml/3 tbsp light soy sauce
15 ml/1 tbsp sugar
15 ml/1 tbsp sunflower oil
1 Chinese lettuce
½ frisée lettuce, torn into bite-size pieces
115 g/4 oz/cup unsalted cashews
2 large carrots, peeled and cut into fine strips
salt and freshly ground black pepper

chicken breast

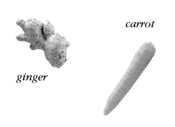

carrot

ginger

cashews

1 Chop the tarragon.

2 Cut the chicken into fine strips and place in a bowl.

3 To make the marinade, mix together in a bowl the tarragon, ginger, soy sauce, sugar and seasoning.

4 Pour the marinade over the chicken strips and leave for 2–4 hours.

5 Strain the chicken from the marinade. Heat the wok, then add the oil. When the oil is hot, stir-fry the chicken for 3 minutes, add the marinade and bubble for 2–3 minutes.

6 Slice the Chinese lettuce and arrange on a plate with the frisée. Toss the cashews and carrots together with the chicken, pile on top of the bed of lettuce and serve immediately.

Sukiyaki-style Beef

This Japanese dish is a meal in itself; the recipe incorporates all the traditional elements – meat, vegetables, noodles and beancurd. If you want to do it all properly, eat the meal with chopsticks, and a spoon to collect the stock juices.

Serves 4

INGREDIENTS
450 g/1 lb thick rump steak
200 g/7 oz Japanese rice noodles
15 ml/1 tbsp shredded suet
200 g/7 oz hard beancurd, cut
   into cubes
8 shitake mushrooms, trimmed
2 medium leeks, sliced into 2.5 cm/
   1 in lengths
90 g/3½ oz baby spinach, to serve

FOR THE STOCK
15 ml/1 tbsp caster sugar
90 ml/6 tbsp rice wine
45 ml/3 tbsp dark soy sauce
125 ml/4 fl oz/½ cup water

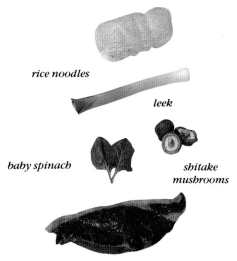

rice noodles

leek

baby spinach

shitake
mushrooms

rump steak

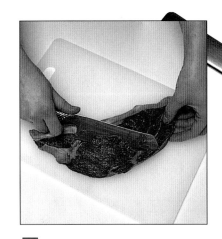

1 Cut the beef into thin slices.

2 Blanch the noodles in boiling water for 2 minutes. Strain well.

3 Mix together all the stock ingredients in a bowl.

4 Heat the wok, then add the suet. When the suet is melted, stir-fry the beef for 2–3 minutes until it is cooked, but still pink in colour.

5 Pour the stock over the beef.

6 Add the remaining ingredients and cook for 4 minutes, until the leeks are tender. Serve a selection of the different ingredients, with a few baby spinach leaves, to each person.

Minted Lamb

Ask your butcher to remove the bone from a leg of
lamb – it is sometimes called a butterfly leg of lamb –
so that the meat can be sliced easily.

Serves 4

INGREDIENTS
450 g/1 lb boneless leg of lamb
30 ml/2 tbsp fresh mint, chopped
½ lemon
300 ml/½ pint/1¼ cups natural low-
    fat yogurt
15 ml/1 tbsp sunflower oil
salt and freshly ground black pepper
lemon wedges and fresh mint sprigs,
    to garnish

lemon

sunflower oil

mint

1 Using a sharp knife, cut the lamb into 6 mm/¼-in thick slices. Place in a bowl.

2 Sprinkle half the mint over the lamb, season well with salt and pepper and leave for 20 minutes.

3 Roughly cut up the lemon and place in the food processor. Process until finely chopped. Empty it into a bowl, then stir in the yogurt and remaining mint.

4 Heat the wok, then add the oil. When the oil is hot, add the lamb and stir-fry for 4–5 minutes until cooked. Serve with the yogurt dressing, garnished with a lemon wedge and fresh mint sprigs.

Chicken Teriyaki

A bowl of boiled rice is the ideal accompaniment to this Japanese-style chicken dish.

Serves 4

INGREDIENTS
450 g/1 lb boneless, skinless
    chicken breasts
orange segments and mustard and
    cress, to garnish

FOR THE MARINADE
5 ml/1 tsp sugar
15 ml/1 tbsp rice wine
15 ml/1 tbsp dry sherry
30 ml/2 tbsp dark soy sauce
rind of 1 orange, grated

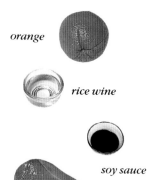

orange

rice wine

soy sauce

chicken breast

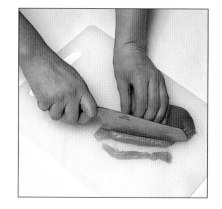

1 Finely slice the chicken.

2 Mix all the marinade ingredients together in a bowl.

COOK'S TIP

Make sure the marinade is brought to the boil and cooked for 4–5 minutes, because it has been in contact with raw chicken.

3 Place the chicken in a bowl, pour over the marinade and leave to marinate for 15 minutes.

4 Heat the wok, add the chicken and marinade and stir-fry for 4–5 minutes. Serve garnished with orange segments and mustard and cress.

Stir-fried Turkey with Broccoli and Mushrooms

This is a really easy, tasty supper dish which works well with chicken too.

Serves 4

INGREDIENTS

115 g/4 oz broccoli florets
4 spring onions
5 ml/1 tsp cornflour
45 ml/3 tbsp oyster sauce
15 ml/1 tbsp dark soy sauce
120 ml/4 fl oz/½ cup
   chicken stock
10 ml/2 tsp lemon juice
45 ml/3 tbsp groundnut oil
450 g/1 lb turkey steaks, cut into
   strips, about 5 mm x 5 cm/
   ¼ x 2 in
1 small onion, chopped
2 garlic cloves, crushed
10 ml/2 tsp grated fresh
   root ginger
115 g/4 oz fresh shiitake
   mushrooms, sliced
75 g/3 oz baby sweetcorn,
   halved lengthways
15 ml/1 tbsp sesame oil
salt and ground black pepper
egg noodles, to serve

onion

broccoli

spring onion

oyster sauce *turkey* *mushrooms*

lemon

dark soy sauce

groundnut oil

baby sweetcorn

garlic

chicken stock

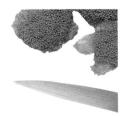

1 Divide the broccoli florets into smaller sprigs and cut the stalks into thin diagonal slices.

2 Finely chop the white parts of the spring onions and slice the green parts into thin shreds.

3 In a bowl, blend together the cornflour, oyster sauce, soy sauce, stock and lemon juice. Set aside.

4 Heat a wok until hot, add 30 ml/ 2 tbsp of the groundnut oil and swirl it around. Add the turkey and stir-fry for about 2 minutes until golden and crispy at the edges. Remove the turkey from the wok and keep warm.

5 Add the remaining groundnut oil to the wok and stir-fry the chopped onion, garlic and ginger over a medium heat for about 1 minute. Increase the heat to high, add the broccoli, mushrooms and sweetcorn and stir-fry for 2 minutes.

6 Return the turkey to the wok, then add the sauce with the chopped spring onion and seasoning. Cook, stirring, for about 1 minute until the sauce has thickened. Stir in the sesame oil. Serve immediately on a bed of egg noodles with the finely shredded spring onion scattered on top.

Thai Red Chicken Curry

Here chicken and potatoes are simmered in spiced coconut milk, then garnished with shredded kaffir lime leaves and red chillies.

Serves 4

INGREDIENTS
1 onion
15 ml/1 tbsp groundnut oil
400 ml/14 fl oz/1⅔ cups
    coconut milk
30 ml/2 tbsp red curry paste
30 ml/2 tbsp Thai fish sauce
    (*nam pla*)
15 ml/1 tbsp soft light
    brown sugar
225 g/8 oz tiny new potatoes
450 g/1 lb skinless chicken
    breasts, cut into chunks
15 ml/1 tbsp lime juice
30 ml/2 tbsp chopped fresh mint
15 ml/1 tbsp chopped fresh basil
2 kaffir lime leaves, shredded
1-2 fresh red chillies, seeded and
    finely shredded
salt and ground black pepper

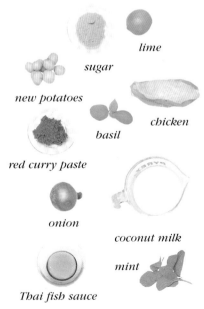

lime
sugar
new potatoes
basil
chicken
red curry paste
onion
coconut milk
mint
Thai fish sauce

VARIATION
You can use boneless chicken thighs instead of breasts. Simply skin them, cut the flesh into chunks and cook in the coconut milk with the potatoes.

1 Cut the onion into wedges.

2 Heat a wok until hot, add the oil and swirl it around. Add the onion and stir-fry for 3–4 minutes.

3 Pour in the coconut milk, then bring to the boil, stirring. Stir in the curry paste, fish sauce and sugar.

4 Add the potatoes and seasoning and simmer gently, covered, for about 20 minutes.

5 Add the chicken chunks and cook, covered, over a low heat for a further 5–10 minutes until the chicken and potatoes are tender.

6 Stir in the lime juice, chopped mint and basil. Serve at once, sprinkled with the shredded kaffir lime leaves and red chillies.

Stir-fried Pork with Lychees

Lychees have a very pretty pink skin which, when peeled, reveals a soft fleshy berry with a hard shiny stone. If you cannot buy fresh lychees, this dish can be made with drained canned lychees.

Serves 4

INGREDIENTS
450 g/1 lb fatty pork, for example belly pork
30 ml/2 tbsp hoisin sauce
4 spring onions, sliced
175 g/6 oz lychees, peeled, stoned and cut into slivers
salt and freshly ground black pepper
fresh lychees and fresh parsley sprigs, to garnish

pork

hoisin sauce

spring onions

lychees

1 Cut the pork into bite-size pieces.

2 Pour the hoisin sauce over the pork and marinate for 30 minutes.

3 Heat the wok, then add the pork and stir-fry for 5 minutes until crisp and golden. Add the spring onions and stir-fry for a further 2 minutes.

4 Scatter the lychee slivers over the pork, and season well with salt and pepper. Garnish with fresh lychees and fresh parsley, and serve.

Oriental Beef

This sumptuously rich beef melts in the mouth, and is perfectly complemented by the cool, crunchy relish.

Serves 4

INGREDIENTS
450 g/1 lb rump steak

FOR THE MARINADE
15 ml/1 tbsp sunflower oil
2 cloves garlic, crushed
60 ml/4 tbsp dark soy sauce
30 ml/2 tbsp dry sherry
10 ml/2 tsp soft dark brown sugar

FOR THE RELISH
6 radishes
10 cm/4 in piece cucumber
1 piece stem ginger
4 whole radishes, to garnish

rump steak

brown sugar

soy sauce

garlic

radish

1 Cut the beef into thin strips. Place in a bowl.

2 To make the marinade, mix together the garlic, soy sauce, sherry and sugar in a bowl. Pour it over the beef and leave to marinate overnight.

3 To make the relish, chop the radishes and cucumber into matchsticks and the ginger into small matchsticks. Mix well together in a bowl.

4 Heat the wok, then add the oil. When the oil is hot, add the meat and marinade and stir-fry for 3–4 minutes. Serve with the relish, and garnish with a whole radish on each plate.

Sweet-sour Duck with Mango

Mango adds natural sweetness to this colourful stir-fry. Crispy deep-fried noodles make the perfect accompaniment.

Serves 4

INGREDIENTS

225–350 g/8–12 oz duck breasts
45 ml/3 tbsp dark soy sauce
15 ml/1 tbsp Chinese rice wine
5 ml/1 tsp sesame oil
5 ml/1 tsp Chinese five-
    spice powder
15 ml/1 tbsp soft brown sugar
10 ml/2 tsp cornflour
45 ml/3 tbsp Chinese rice vinegar
15 ml/1 tbsp tomato ketchup
1 mango, not too ripe
3 baby aubergines
1 red onion
1 carrot
60 ml/4 tbsp groundnut oil
1 garlic clove, sliced
2.5 cm/1 in piece fresh root
    ginger, cut into shreds
75 g/3 oz sugar snap peas

1 Thinly slice the duck breasts and place in a bowl. Mix together 15 ml/ 1 tbsp of the soy sauce with the rice wine or sherry, sesame oil and five-spice powder. Pour over the duck, cover and leave to marinate for 1–2 hours. In a separate bowl, blend together the sugar, cornflour, rice vinegar, ketchup and remaining soy sauce. Set aside.

2 Peel the mango, slice the flesh from the stone, then cut into thick strips. Slice the aubergines, onion and carrot into similar-sized pieces.

3 Heat a wok until hot, add 30 ml/ 2 tbsp of the oil and swirl it around. Drain the duck, reserving the marinade. Stir-fry the duck slices over a high heat until the fat is crisp and golden. Remove and keep warm. Add 15 ml/1 tbsp of the oil to the wok and stir-fry the aubergine for 3 minutes until golden.

duck breasts

groundnut oil

carrot

dark soy sauce

aubergines

Chinese rice wine

mango

sesame oil

sugar snap peas

tomato ketchup

ginger

sugar

red onion

garlic

Chinese five-spice powder

4 Add the remaining oil and fry the onion, garlic, ginger and carrot for 2–3 minutes, then add the sugar snap peas and stir-fry for a further 2 minutes.

5 Add the mango and return the duck with the sauce and reserved marinade to the wok. Cook, stirring, until the sauce thickens slightly. Serve at once.

Stir-fried Pork with Mustard

Fry the apples for this dish very carefully, because they will disintegrate if they are overcooked.

Serves 4

INGREDIENTS

500 g/1¼ lb pork fillet
1 tart apple, such as Granny Smith
40 g/1½ oz/3 tbsp unsalted butter
15 ml/1 tbsp caster sugar
1 small onion, finely chopped
30 ml/2 tbsp Calvados or
    other brandy
15 ml/1 tbsp Meaux or coarse-grain
    mustard
150 ml/¼ pint/⅔ cup double cream
30 ml/2 tbsp fresh parsley, chopped
salt and freshly ground black pepper
flat-leaf parsley sprigs, to garnish

pork fillet

onion

mustard

apple

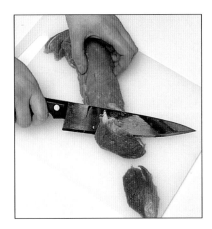

1 Cut the pork fillet into thin slices.

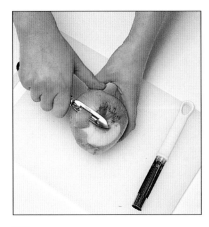

2 Peel and core the apple. Cut it into thick slices.

3 Heat the wok, then add half the butter. When the butter is hot, add the apple slices, sprinkle over the sugar, and stir-fry for 2–3 minutes. Remove the apple and set aside. Wipe out the wok with kitchen towels.

4 Heat the wok, then add the remaining butter and stir-fry the pork fillet and onion together for 2–3 minutes, until the pork is golden and the onion has begun to soften.

5 Stir in the Calvados or other brandy and boil until it is reduced by half. Stir in the mustard.

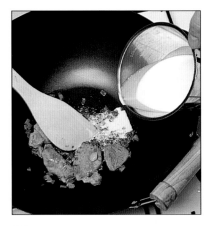

6 Add the cream and simmer for about 1 minute, then stir in the parsley. Serve garnished with sprigs of flat-leaf parsley.

Buffalo-style Chicken Wings

This fiery-hot fried chicken recipe is said to have originated in the town of Buffalo, New York, but is now popular throughout the USA. Serve it with traditional Blue-cheese Dip and celery sticks.

Makes 48

INGREDIENTS
24 plump chicken wings, tips
  removed
vegetable oil, for frying
salt
75 g/3 oz butter
50 ml/2 oz/¼ cup hot pepper sauce,
  or to taste
15 ml/1 tbsp white or cider vinegar

FOR THE BLUE-CHEESE DIP
115 g/4 oz blue cheese, such as
  Danish blue
120ml/4 fl oz/½ cup mayonnaise
120 ml/4 fl oz/½ cup sour cream
2–3 spring onions, finely chopped
1 garlic clove, finely chopped
15 ml/1 tbsp white or cider vinegar
celery sticks, to serve

1 To make the dip, use a fork to gently mash the blue cheese against the side of a bowl. Add the mayonnaise, sour cream, spring onions, garlic and vinegar and stir together until well blended. Refrigerate until ready to serve.

spring onions
Danish blue cheese
sour cream
vegetable oil
white vinegar
chicken wings
mayonnaise
butter
hot pepper sauce

2 Using kitchen scissors or a sharp knife, cut each wing in half at the joint to make 48 pieces in all.

3 In a large saucepan or wok, heat 5 cm/2 in of oil until hot but not smoking. Fry the chicken wing pieces in small batches for 8–10 minutes until crisp and golden, turning once. Drain on paper towels. Season and arrange in a bowl.

4 In a small saucepan over medium-low heat, melt the butter. Stir in the hot-pepper sauce and vinegar and immediately pour over the chicken, tossing to combine. Serve hot with the blue-cheese dip and celery sticks.

Cellophane Noodles with Pork

Unlike other types of noodle, cellophane noodles can be successfully reheated.

Serves 3-4

INGREDIENTS

115 g/4 oz cellophane noodles
4 dried Chinese black mushrooms
225 g/8 oz boneless lean pork
30 ml/2 tbsp dark soy sauce
30 ml/2 tbsp Chinese rice wine
2 garlic cloves, crushed
15 ml/1 tbsp grated fresh
  root ginger
5 ml/1 tsp chilli oil
45 ml/3 tbsp groundnut oil
4-6 spring onions, chopped
5 ml/1 tsp cornflour blended
  with 175 ml/6 fl oz/¾ cup
  chicken stock or water
30 ml/2 tbsp chopped
  fresh coriander
salt and ground black pepper
coriander sprigs, to garnish

spring onions

noodles

chicken stock *Chinese rice wine*

mushrooms

dark soy sauce

pork

chilli oil *groundnut oil*

1 Put the noodles and mushrooms in separate bowls and pour over warm water to cover. Leave to soak for 15–20 minutes until soft; drain well. Cut the noodles into 12.5 cm/5 in lengths using scissors or a knife. Squeeze out any water from the mushrooms, discard the stems and then finely chop the caps.

2 Meanwhile, cut the pork into very small cubes. Put into a bowl with the soy sauce, rice wine, garlic, ginger and chilli oil, then leave for about 15 minutes. Drain, reserving the marinade.

3 Heat a wok until hot, add the oil and swirl it around. Add the pork and mushrooms and stir-fry for 3 minutes. Add the spring onions and stir-fry for 1 minute. Stir in the cornflour, marinade and seasoning. Cook for about 1 minute.

4 Add the noodles and stir-fry for about 2 minutes until the noodles absorb most of the liquid and the pork is cooked through. Stir in the chopped coriander. Taste and adjust the seasoning. Serve garnished with coriander sprigs.

Sizzling Beef with Celeriac Straw

The crisp celeriac matchsticks look like fine pieces of straw when cooked and have a mild celery-like flavour that is quite delicious.

Serves 4

INGREDIENTS
450 g/1 lb celeriac
150 ml/¼ pint/⅔ cup vegetable oil
1 red pepper
6 spring onions
450 g/1 lb rump steak
60 ml/4 tbsp beef stock
30 ml/2 tbsp sherry vinegar
10 ml/2 tsp Worcestershire sauce
10 ml/2 tsp tomato purée
salt and freshly ground black pepper

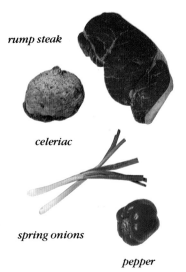

rump steak

celeriac

spring onions

pepper

1 Peel the celeriac and then cut it into fine matchsticks, using a cleaver.

2 Heat the wok, then add two-thirds of the oil. When the oil is hot, fry the celeriac matchsticks in batches until golden brown and crispy. Drain well on kitchen towels.

3 Chop the red pepper and the spring onions into 2.5 cm/1 in lengths, using diagonal cuts.

4 Chop the beef into strips, across the grain of the meat.

5 Heat the wok, and then add the remaining oil. When the oil is hot, stir-fry the chopped spring onions and red pepper for 2–3 minutes.

6 Add the beef strips and stir-fry for a further 3–4 minutes until well browned. Add the stock, vinegar, Worcestershire sauce and tomato purée. Season well and serve with the celeriac straw.

Turkey with Sage, Prunes and Brandy

This stir-fry has a very rich sauce based on a good brandy – use the best you can afford.

Serves 4

INGREDIENTS

115 g/4 oz prunes
1.5 kg/3–3½ lb turkey breast
300 ml/½ pint/1¼ cups cognac
   or brandy
15 ml/1 tbsp fresh sage, chopped
150 g/5 oz smoked bacon, in
   one piece
50 g/2 oz/4 tbsp butter
24 baby onions, peeled and quartered
salt and freshly ground black pepper
fresh sage sprigs, to garnish

smoked bacon

prunes

baby onion

sage

1 Stone the prunes and cut them into slivers. Remove the skin from the turkey and cut the breast into thin pieces.

2 Mix together the prunes, turkey, cognac and sage in a non-metallic dish. Cover and leave to marinate overnight.

3 Next day, strain the turkey and prunes, reserving the cognac mixture, and pat dry on kitchen towels.

4 Cut the bacon into lardons (dice).

5 Heat the wok and add half the butter. When melted, add the onions and stir-fry for 4 minutes until crisp and golden. Set aside.

6 Heat the wok, add the lardons and stir-fry for 1 minute until the bacon begins to release some fat. Add the remaining butter and stir-fry the turkey and prunes for 3–4 minutes until crisp and golden. Push the turkey mixture to one side in the wok, add the cognac and simmer until thickened. Stir the turkey into the sauce, season well with salt and ground black pepper, and serve garnished with sage.

Glazed Lamb

Lemon and honey make a classically good combination in sweet dishes, and this lamb recipe shows how well they work together in savoury dishes, too. Serve with a fresh mixed salad to complete this delicious dish.

Serves 4

INGREDIENTS
450 g/1 lb boneless lean lamb
15 ml/1 tbsp grapeseed oil
175 g/6 oz mangetout peas, topped
 and tailed
3 spring onions, sliced
30 ml/2 tbsp clear honey
juice of half a lemon
30 ml/2 tbsp fresh coriander, chopped
15 ml/1 tbsp sesame seeds
salt and freshly ground black pepper

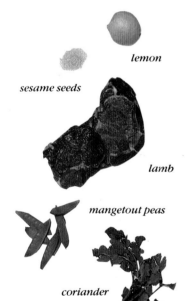

lemon

sesame seeds

lamb

mangetout peas

coriander

1 Using a sharp knife, cut the lamb into thin strips.

2 Heat the wok, then add the oil. When the oil is hot, stir-fry the lamb until browned all over. Remove from the wok and keep warm.

3 Add the mangetout peas and spring onions to the hot wok and stir-fry for 30 seconds.

4 Return the lamb to the wok and add the honey, lemon juice, coriander and sesame seeds, and season well. Bring to the boil and bubble for 1 minute until the lamb is well coated in the honey mixture.

Spicy Beef

Promoting a fast-growing trend in worldwide cuisine, the wok is used in this recipe to produce a colourful and healthy meal.

Serves 4

INGREDIENTS
15 ml/1 tbsp oil
450 g/1 lb/4 cups minced beef
2.5 cm/1 in fresh root ginger, sliced
5 ml/1 tsp Chinese five-spice powder
1 red chilli, sliced
50 g/2 oz mangetout
1 red pepper, seeded and chopped
1 carrot, sliced
115 g/4 oz beansprouts
15 ml/1 tbsp sesame oil

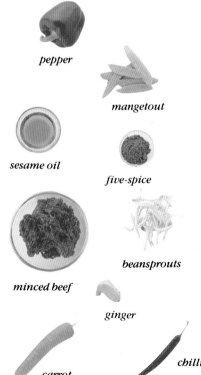

pepper

mangetout

sesame oil

five-spice

beansprouts

minced beef

ginger

carrot

chilli

1 Heat the oil in a wok until almost smoking. Add the minced beef and cook for 3 minutes, stirring all the time.

2 Add the ginger, Chinese five-spice powder and chilli. Cook for 1 minute.

3 Add the mangetout, pepper and carrot and cook for a further 3 minutes, stirring continuously.

4 Add the beansprouts and sesame oil and cook for a final 2 minutes. Serve immediately with noodles.

Stir-fried Sweet and Sour Chicken

There are few cookery concepts that are better suited to today's busy lifestyle than the all-in-one stir-fry. This one has a South-east Asian influence.

Serves 4

INGREDIENTS
275 g/10 oz Chinese egg noodles
30 ml/2 tbsp vegetable oil
3 spring onions, chopped
1 garlic clove, crushed
2.5 cm/1 in fresh root ginger, peeled and grated
5 ml/1 tsp hot paprika
5 ml/1 tsp ground coriander
3 boneless chicken breasts, sliced
115 g/4 oz/1 cup sugar-snap peas, topped and tailed
115 g/4 oz baby sweetcorn, halved
225 g/8 oz fresh beansprouts
15 ml/1 tbsp cornflour
45 ml/3 tbsp soy sauce
45 ml/3 tbsp lemon juice
15 ml/1 tbsp sugar
45 ml/3 tbsp chopped fresh coriander or spring onion tops, to garnish

COOK'S TIP

Large wok lids are cumbersome and can be difficult to store in a small kitchen. Consider placing a circle of greaseproof paper against the food surface to keep cooking juices in.

1 Bring a large saucepan of salted water to the boil. Add the noodles and cook according to the packet instructions. Drain, cover and keep warm.

chicken breasts
garlic
spring onions
paprika
soy sauce
egg noodles
sugar-snap peas
ginger

2 Heat the oil. Add the spring onions and cook over a gentle heat. Mix in the next five ingredients, then stir-fry for 3–4 minutes. Add the next three ingredients and steam briefly. Add the noodles.

3 Combine the cornflour, soy sauce, lemon juice and sugar in a small bowl. Add to the wok and simmer briefly to thicken. Serve garnished with chopped coriander or spring onion tops.

Stir-fried Beef and Broccoli

This spicy beef may be served with noodles or on a bed of boiled rice for a speedy and low calorie Chinese meal.

Serves 4

INGREDIENTS

350 g/12 oz rump or lean prime
    casserole steak
15 ml/1 tbsp cornflour
5 ml/1 tsp sesame oil
350 g/12 oz broccoli, cut into
    small florets
4 spring onions, sliced on the diagonal
1 carrot, cut into matchstick strips
1 garlic clove, crushed
2.5 cm/1 in piece root ginger, cut into
    very fine strips
120 ml/4 fl oz/½ cup beef stock
30 ml/2 tbsp soy sauce
30 ml/2 tbsp dry sherry
10 ml/2 tsp soft light brown sugar
spring onion tassels, to garnish
noodles or rice, to serve

steak

spring onions

ginger

broccoli

garlic

carrot

1 Trim the beef and cut into thin slices across the grain. Cut each slice into thin strips. Toss in the cornflour to coat thoroughly.

2 Heat the sesame oil in a large non-stick frying pan or wok. Add the beef strips and stir-fry over a brisk heat for 3 minutes. Remove and set aside.

COOK'S TIP

To make spring onion tassels, trim the bulb base then cut the green shoot so that the onion is 7.5 cm/3 in long. Shred to within 2.5 cm/1 in of the base and put into iced water for 1 hour.

3 Add the broccoli, spring onions, carrot, garlic clove, ginger and stock to the frying pan or wok. Cover and simmer for 3 minutes. Uncover and cook, stirring until all the stock has reduced entirely.

4 Mix the soy sauce, sherry and brown sugar together. Add to the frying pan or wok with the beef. Cook for 2–3 minutes stirring continuously. Spoon into a warm serving dish and garnish with spring onion tassels. Serve on a bed of noodles or rice.

Stir-fried Parsnips

Serve these sweet and piquant parsnips as an accompaniment to roast beef or as a vegetarian starter for two.

Serves 4 as an accompaniment

INGREDIENTS
2 large cloves garlic
350 g/12 oz parsnips
15 ml/1 tbsp vegetable oil
2.5 cm/1 in piece root ginger, peeled and grated
rind of 1 lime, grated
45 ml/3 tbsp clear honey
salt and freshly ground black pepper

lime

ginger

garlic

parsnip

1 Peel and cut the garlic into slices.

2 Peel and cut the parsnips into long, thin strands.

3 Heat the wok, then swirl in the oil. When the oil is hot, stir-fry the parsnips for 2 minutes.

4 Sprinkle the ginger, lime rind, salt and pepper and honey over the parsnips. Stir to coat the vegetables and serve.

Stir-fried Spinach with Garlic and Sesame Seeds

The sesame seeds add a crunchy texture which contrasts well with the wilted spinach in this easy vegetable dish.

Serves 2

INGREDIENTS
225 g/8 oz fresh spinach, washed
25 ml/1½ tbsp sesame seeds
30 ml/2 tbsp groundnut oil
1.5 ml/¼ tsp sea salt flakes
2–3 garlic cloves, sliced

spinach

groundnut oil

garlic

sesame seeds

1 Shake the spinach to get rid of any excess water, then remove the stalks and discard any yellow or damaged leaves. Lay several spinach leaves one on top of another, roll up tightly and cut crossways into wide strips. Repeat with the remaining leaves.

2 Heat a wok to a medium heat, add the sesame seeds and dry fry, stirring, for 1–2 minutes until golden brown. Transfer to a small bowl and set aside.

3 Add the oil to the wok and swirl it around. When hot, add the salt, spinach and garlic and stir-fry for 2 minutes until the spinach just wilts and the leaves are coated with the oil.

4 Sprinkle over the sesame seeds and toss well. Serve at once.

COOK'S TIP
Take care when adding the spinach to the hot oil as it will spit furiously.

Stir-fried Vegetables with Coriander Omelette

This is a great supper dish for vegetarians. The glaze is added here only to make the mixture shine, it is not intended as a sauce.

Serves 3-4

INGREDIENTS
FOR THE OMELETTE
2 eggs
30 ml/2 tbsp water
45 ml/3 tbsp chopped
   fresh coriander
salt and ground black pepper
15 ml/1 tbsp groundnut oil

FOR THE GLAZED VEGETABLES
15 ml/1 tbsp cornflour
30 ml/2 tbsp dry sherry
15 ml/1 tbsp sweet chilli sauce
120 ml/4 fl oz/½ cup
   vegetable stock
30 ml/2 tbsp groundnut oil
5 ml/1 tsp grated fresh
   root ginger
6-8 spring onions, sliced
115 g/4 oz mange-touts
1 yellow pepper, seeded
   and sliced
115 g/4 oz fresh shiitake or
   button mushrooms
75 g/3 oz (drained weight)
   canned water chestnuts, rinsed
115 g/4 oz beansprouts
½ small Chinese cabbage,
   coarsely shredded

1 Make the omelette: whisk the eggs, water, coriander and seasoning in a small bowl. Heat the oil in a wok. Pour in the eggs, then tilt the wok so that the mixture spreads to an even layer. Cook over a high heat until the edges are slightly crisp.

2 With a wok spatula or palette knife, flip the omelette over and cook the other side for about 30 seconds until lightly browned. Turn the omelette on to a board and leave to cool. When cold, roll up loosely and cut into thin slices. Wipe the wok clean.

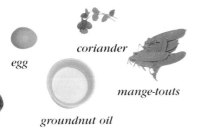

coriander

egg

mange-touts

groundnut oil

spring onion

mushrooms

yellow pepper

stock

sweet chilli sauce

Chinese cabbage

beansprouts

3 In a bowl, blend together the cornflour, soy sauce, chilli sauce and stock. Set aside.

4 Heat the wok until hot, add the oil and swirl it around, add the ginger and spring onions and stir-fry for a few seconds to flavour the oil. Add the mange-touts, pepper, mushrooms and water chestnuts and stir-fry for 3 minutes.

VARIATION
Vary the combination of vegetables used according to availability and taste.

5 Add the beansprouts and Chinese cabbage and stir-fry for 2 minutes.

6 Pour in the glaze ingredients and cook, stirring, for about 1 minute until the glaze thickens and coats the vegetables. Turn the vegetables on to a warmed serving plate and top with the omelette shreds. Serve at once.

Crispy Cabbage

This makes a wonderful accompaniment to meat or vegetable dishes – just a couple of spoonfuls will add crispy texture to a meal. It goes especially well with prawn dishes.

Serves 2–4 as an accompaniment

INGREDIENTS
4 juniper berries
1 large Savoy cabbage
60 ml/4 tbsp vegetable oil
1 clove garlic, crushed
5 ml/1 tsp caster sugar
5 ml/1 tsp salt

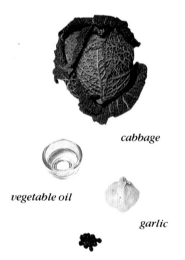

cabbage

vegetable oil

garlic

juniper berries

1 Finely crush the juniper berries, using a pestle and mortar.

2 Finely shred the cabbage.

3 Heat the wok, then add the oil. When the oil is hot, stir-fry the garlic for 1 minute. Add the cabbage and stir-fry for 3–4 minutes until crispy. Remove and pat dry with kitchen towels.

4 Return the cabbage to the wok. Toss the cabbage in sugar, salt and crushed juniper berries and serve hot or cold.

Szechuan Aubergines

This dish is also known as fish-fragrant aubergine, as the aubergine is cooked with flavourings that are often used with fish.

Serves 4

INGREDIENTS
2 small aubergines
5 ml/1 tsp salt
3 dried red chillies
groundnut oil, for deep frying
3–4 garlic cloves, finely chopped
1 cm/½ in piece fresh root ginger, finely chopped
4 spring onions, cut into 2.5 cm/ 1 in lengths (white and green parts separated)
15 ml/1 tbsp Chinese rice wine or medium-dry sherry
15 ml/1 tbsp light soy sauce
5 ml/1 tsp sugar
1.5 ml/¼ tsp ground roasted Szechuan peppercorns
15 ml/1 tbsp Chinese rice vinegar
5 ml/1 tsp sesame oil

ginger

aubergine

dried red chillies

spring onions

Chinese rice wine

light soy sauce

sesame oil

garlic

groundnut oil

1 Trim the aubergines and cut into strips, about 4 cm/1½ in wide and 7.5 cm/3 in long. Place the aubergines in a colander and sprinkle over the salt. Leave for 30 minutes, then rinse them thoroughly under cold running water. Pat dry with kitchen paper.

2 Meanwhile, soak the chillies in warm water for 15 minutes. Drain, then cut each chilli into three or four pieces, discarding the seeds.

3 Half-fill a wok with oil and heat to 180°C/350°F. Deep fry the aubergine until golden brown. Drain on kitchen paper. Pour off most of the oil from the wok. Reheat the oil and add the garlic, ginger and white spring onion.

4 Stir-fry for 30 seconds. Add the aubergine and toss, then add the rice wine or sherry, soy sauce, sugar, ground Szechuan peppercorns and rice vinegar. Stir-fry for 1–2 minutes. Sprinkle over the sesame oil and green spring onion.

Spiced Vegetables with Coconut

This spicy and substantial dish could be served as a starter, or as a vegetarian main course for two. Eat it with spoons and forks, and hunks of granary bread for mopping up the delicious coconut milk.

Serves 2–4 as a starter

INGREDIENTS
1 red chilli
2 large carrots
6 stalks celery
1 bulb fennel
30 ml/2 tbsp grapeseed oil
2.5 cm/1 in piece root ginger, peeled and grated
1 clove garlic, crushed
3 spring onions, sliced
1 × 400 ml/14 fl oz can thin coconut milk
15 ml/1 tbsp fresh coriander, chopped
salt and freshly ground black pepper
coriander sprigs, to garnish

celery

spring onions

fennel

carrot

1 Halve, deseed and finely chop the chilli. If necessary, wear rubber gloves to protect your hands.

2 Slice the carrots on the diagonal. Slice the celery stalks on the diagonal.

3 Trim the fennel head and slice roughly, using a sharp knife.

4 Heat the wok, then add the oil. When the oil is hot, add the ginger and garlic, chilli, carrots, celery, fennel and spring onions and stir-fry for 2 minutes.

5 Stir in the coconut milk with a large spoon and bring to the boil.

6 Stir in the coriander and salt and pepper, and serve garnished with coriander sprigs.

Chinese Greens with Oyster Sauce

Here Chinese greens are prepared in a very simple way – stir-fried and served with oyster sauce. The combination makes a simple, quickly prepared, tasty accompaniment.

Serves 3-4

INGREDIENTS
450 g/1 lb Chinese greens
    (*pak choi*)
30 ml/2 tbsp groundnut oil
15–30 ml/1–2 tbsp oyster sauce

Chinese greens

groundnut oil

oyster sauce

1 Trim the Chinese greens, removing any discoloured leaves and damaged stems. Tear into manageable pieces.

2 Heat a wok until hot, add the oil and swirl it around.

3 Add the Chinese greens and stir-fry for 2–3 minutes until the greens have wilted a little.

4 Add the oyster sauce and continue to stir-fry a few seconds more until the greens are cooked but still slightly crisp. Serve immediately.

VARIATION
You can replace the Chinese greens with Chinese flowering cabbage, which is also known by its Cantonese name *choi sam*. It has bright green leaves and tiny yellow flowers, which are also eaten along with the leaves and stalks. It is available from oriental grocers.

Deep-fried Root Vegetables with Spiced Salt

All kinds of root vegetables may be finely sliced and deep-fried to make "crisps". Serve as an accompaniment to an oriental-style meal or simply by themselves as a nibble.

Serves 4–6

INGREDIENTS
1 carrot
2 parsnips
2 raw beetroots
1 sweet potato
groundnut oil, for deep frying
1.5 ml/¼ tsp chilli powder
5 ml/1 tsp sea salt flakes

chilli powder

sweet potato

groundnut oil

beetroot

carrot

parsnips

1 Peel all the vegetables, then slice the carrot and parsnips into long, thin ribbons and the beetroots and sweet potato into thin rounds. Pat dry on kitchen paper.

2 Half-fill a wok with oil and heat to 180°C/350°F. Add the vegetable slices in batches and deep-fry for 2–3 minutes until golden and crisp. Remove and drain on kitchen paper.

3 Place the chilli powder and sea salt in a mortar and grind together to a coarse powder.

4 Pile up the vegetable "crisps" on a serving plate and sprinkle over the spiced salt.

COOK'S TIP
To save time you can slice the vegetables using a mandoline or a blender or food processor with a thin slicing disc attached.

Yellow Flower Vegetables

To serve, each person spreads hoisin sauce on a pancake, adds filling and rolls it up.

Serves 4

INGREDIENTS
3 eggs
30 ml/2 tbsp water
60 ml/4 tbsp groundnut oil
25 g/1 oz dried Chinese
  black mushrooms
25 g/1 oz dried wood ears
10 ml/2 tsp cornflour
30 ml/2 tbsp light soy sauce
30 ml/2 tbsp Chinese rice wine
  or medium-dry sherry
10 ml/2 tsp sesame oil
2 garlic cloves, finely chopped
1 cm/½ in piece fresh root ginger,
  cut into thin shreds
75 g/3 oz canned sliced bamboo
  shoots (drained weight), rinsed
175 g/6 oz beansprouts
4 spring onions, finely shredded
salt and ground black pepper
Chinese pancakes and hoisin
  sauce, to serve

COOK'S TIP
Chinese pancakes are available from oriental grocers. Reheat them in a bamboo steamer for 2–3 minutes before serving.

1 Whisk the eggs, water and seasoning in a small bowl. Heat 15 ml/ 1 tbsp of the groundnut oil in a wok and swirl it around. Pour in the eggs, then tilt the wok so that they spread to an even layer. Continue to cook over a high heat for about 2 minutes until set. Turn on to a board and, when cool, roll up and cut into thin strips. Wipe the wok clean.

2 Meanwhile, put the black mushrooms and wood ears into separate bowls. Pour over enough warm water to cover, then leave to soak for 20–30 minutes until soft. Drain the dried mushrooms, reserving their soaking liquid. Squeeze the excess liquid from each of them.

3 Remove the tough stalks and thinly slice the black mushrooms. Finely shred the wood ears. Set aside. Strain the reserved soaking liquid through muslin into a jug; reserve 120 ml/4 fl oz/½ cup of the liquid. In a bowl, blend the cornflour with the reserved liquid, soy sauce, rice wine or sherry and sesame oil.

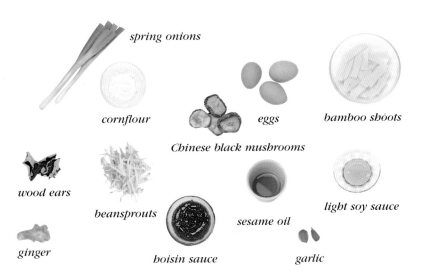

spring onions

cornflour

eggs

bamboo shoots

Chinese black mushrooms

wood ears

beansprouts

sesame oil

light soy sauce

ginger

hoisin sauce

garlic

4 Heat the wok over a medium heat, add the remaining groundnut oil and swirl it around. Add the wood ears and black mushrooms and stir-fry for about 2 minutes. Add the garlic, ginger, bamboo shoots and beansprouts and stir-fry for 1–2 minutes.

5 Pour in the cornflour mixture and cook, stirring, for 1 minute until thickened. Add the spring onions and omelette strips and toss gently. Adjust the seasoning, adding more soy sauce, if needed. Serve at once with the Chinese pancakes and hoisin sauce.

Spicy Vegetable Fritters with Thai Salsa

The Thai salsa goes just as well with plain stir-fried salmon strips or stir-fried beef as it does with these courgette fritters.

Serves 2–4 as a starter

INGREDIENTS
10 ml/2 tsp cumin seeds
10 ml/2 tsp coriander seeds
450 g/1 lb courgettes
115 g/4 oz/1 cup chickpea
  (gram) flour
2.5 ml/½ tsp bicarbonate of soda
125 ml/4 fl oz/½ cup groundnut oil
fresh mint sprigs, to garnish

FOR THE THAI SALSA
½ cucumber, diced
3 spring onions, chopped
6 radishes, cubed
30 ml/2 tbsp fresh mint, chopped
2.5 cm/1 in piece root ginger, peeled
  and grated
45 ml/3 tbsp lime juice
30 ml/2 tbsp caster sugar
3 cloves garlic, crushed

cucumber

mint   *ginger*

radishes

courgette

1 Heat the wok, then toast the cumin and coriander seeds. Cool them, then grind well, using a pestle and mortar.

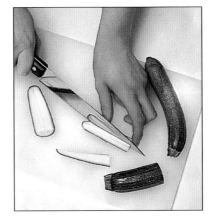

2 Cut the courgettes into 7.5 cm/3 in sticks. Place in a bowl.

3 Blend the flour, bicarbonate of soda, spices and salt and pepper in a food processor. Add 125 ml/4 fl oz warm water with 15 ml/1 tbsp groundnut oil, and blend again.

4 Coat the courgettes in the batter, then leave to stand for 10 minutes.

5 To make the Thai salsa, mix all the ingredients together in a bowl.

6 Heat the wok, then add the remaining oil. When the oil is hot, stir-fry the courgettes in batches. Drain well on kitchen towels, then serve hot with the salsa, garnished with fresh mint sprigs.

Spiced Coconut Mushrooms

Here is a simple and delicious way to cook mushrooms. They may be served with almost any Asian meal as well as with grilled or roasted meats and poultry.

Serves 3-4

INGREDIENTS

30 ml/2 tbsp groundnut oil
2 garlic cloves, finely chopped
2 fresh red chillies, seeded and
  sliced into rings
3 shallots, finely chopped
225 g/8 oz brown-cap
  mushrooms, thickly sliced
150 ml/¼ pint/⅔ cup coconut milk
30 ml/2 tbsp chopped fresh
  coriander
salt and ground black pepper

red chillies

coconut milk

mushrooms

groundnut oil

garlic

coriander

1 Heat a wok until hot, add the oil and swirl it around. Add the garlic and chillies, then stir-fry for a few seconds.

2 Add the shallots and stir-fry for 2–3 minutes until softened. Add the mushrooms and stir-fry for 3 minutes.

3 Pour in the coconut milk and bring to the boil. Boil rapidly over a high heat until the liquid is reduced by half and coats the mushrooms. Taste and adjust the seasoning, if necessary.

4 Sprinkle over the coriander and toss gently to mix. Serve at once.

VARIATION
Use snipped fresh chives instead of coriander if you wish.

Marinated Mixed Vegetables with Basil Oil

Basil oil is a must for drizzling over plain stir-fried vegetables. Once it has been made up, it will keep in the fridge for up to 2 weeks.

Serves 2–4 as an accompaniment

INGREDIENTS
15 ml/1 tbsp olive oil
1 clove garlic, crushed
rind of 1 lemon, finely grated
1 × 400 g/14 oz can artichoke hearts, drained
2 large leeks, sliced
225 g/8 oz patty pan squash, halved if large
115 g/4 oz plum tomatoes, cut into segments lengthwise
15 g/½ oz basil leaves
150 ml/¼ pint/⅔ cup olive oil
salt and freshly ground black pepper

patty pan squash

artichoke hearts

leek

plum tomatoes

1 Mix together the olive oil, garlic and lemon rind in a bowl, to make a marinade.

2 Place the artichokes, leeks, patty pan squash and plum tomatoes in a large bowl, pour over the marinade and leave for 30 minutes.

3 Meanwhile, make the basil oil. Blend the basil leaves with the extra-virgin olive oil in a food processor until puréed.

4 Heat the wok, then stir-fry the marinated vegetables for 3–4 minutes, tossing well. Drizzle the basil oil over the vegetables and serve.

Spicy Potatoes and Cauliflower

This dish is simplicity itself to make and may be eaten as a vegetarian main meal for two with Indian breads or rice, a raita, such as cucumber and yogurt, and a fresh mint relish.

Serves 2

INGREDIENTS
225 g/8 oz potatoes
75 ml/5 tbsp groundnut oil
5 ml/1 tsp ground cumin
5 ml/1 tsp ground coriander
1.5 ml/¼ tsp ground turmeric
1.5 ml/¼ tsp cayenne pepper
1 fresh green chilli, seeded and
   finely chopped
1 medium cauliflower, broken up
   into small florets
5 ml/1 tsp cumin seeds
2 garlic cloves, cut into shreds
15-30 ml/1-2 tbsp chopped
   fresh coriander
salt, to taste

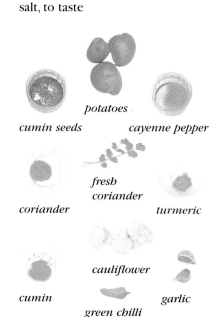

potatoes

cumin seeds   *cayenne pepper*

coriander   *fresh coriander*

turmeric

cauliflower

cumin   *garlic*

green chilli

1 Boil the potatoes in their skins in boiling salted water for about 20 minutes until just tender. Drain and leave to cool. When cool enough to handle, peel and cut into 2.5 cm/1 in cubes.

2 Heat 45 ml/3 tbsp of the oil in a karahi or wok. When hot, add the ground cumin, coriander, turmeric, cayenne pepper and chilli. Let the spices sizzle for a few seconds.

3 Add the cauliflower and about 60 ml/4 tbsp water. Cook, stirring, for 6–8 minutes over a medium heat. Add the potatoes and stir-fry for 2–3 minutes. Season to taste. Remove from the heat.

4 Heat the remaining oil in a small frying pan. When hot, add the cumin seeds and garlic and cook until lightly browned. Pour the mixture over the vegetables. Sprinkle with the chopped fresh coriander and serve at once.

Stir-fried Chickpeas

Buy canned chickpeas and you will save all the time needed for soaking and then thoroughly cooking dried chickpeas. Served with a crisp green salad, this dish makes a filling vegetarian main course for two, or could be served in smaller quantities as a starter.

Serves 2–4 as an accompaniment

INGREDIENTS
30 ml/2 tbsp sunflower seeds
1 × 400 g/14 oz can chickpeas, drained
5 ml/1 tsp chilli powder
5 ml/1 tsp paprika
30 ml/2 tbsp vegetable oil
1 clove garlic, crushed
200 g/7 oz canned chopped tomatoes
225 g/8 oz fresh spinach, coarse stalks removed
salt and freshly ground black pepper
10 ml/2 tsp chilli oil

spinach

garlic

sunflower seeds

chickpeas

1 Heat the wok, and then add the sunflower seeds. Dry-fry until the seeds are golden and toasted.

2 Remove the sunflower seeds and set aside. Toss the chickpeas in chilli powder and paprika. Remove and reserve.

3 Heat the wok, then add the oil. When the oil is hot, stir-fry the garlic for 30 seconds, add the chickpeas and stir-fry for 1 minute.

4 Stir in the tomatoes and stir-fry for 4 minutes. Toss in the spinach, season well and stir-fry for 1 minute. Drizzle chilli oil and scatter sunflower seeds over the vegetables, then serve.

Red-cooked Tofu with Chinese Mushrooms

Red-cooked is a term applied to Chinese dishes cooked with dark soy sauce. This tasty dish can be served as either a side dish or main meal.

Serves 2-4

INGREDIENTS
225 g/8 oz firm tofu
45 ml/3 tbsp dark soy sauce
30 ml/2 tbsp Chinese rice wine
  or medium-dry sherry
10 ml/2 tsp soft dark brown sugar
1 garlic clove, crushed
15 ml/1 tbsp grated fresh
  root ginger
2.5 ml/½ tsp Chinese five-
  spice powder
pinch of ground roasted
  Szechuan peppercorns
6 dried Chinese black mushrooms
5 ml/1 tsp cornflour
30 ml/2 tbsp groundnut oil
5-6 spring onions, sliced into
  2.5 cm/1 in lengths
rice noodles, to serve
small basil leaves, to garnish

1 Drain the tofu, pat dry with kitchen paper and cut into 2.5cm/1in cubes. Place in a shallow dish. In a small bowl, mix together the soy sauce, rice wine or sherry, sugar, garlic, ginger, five-spice powder and Szechuan peppercorns. Pour the marinade over the tofu, toss well and leave to marinate for about 30 minutes. Drain, reserving the marinade.

2 Meanwhile, soak the dried black mushrooms in warm water for 20–30 minutes until soft. Drain, reserving 90 ml/6 tbsp of the soaking liquid. Squeeze out any excess liquid from the mushrooms, remove the tough stalks and slice the caps. In a small bowl, blend the cornflour with the reserved marinade and mushroom soaking liquid.

3 Heat a wok until hot, add the oil and swirl it around. Add the tofu and fry for 2–3 minutes until evenly golden. Remove from the wok and set aside.

spring onions

Chinese black mushrooms

garlic

tofu

ginger

Chinese five-spice powder

dark soy sauce

Chinese rice wine

Szechuan peppercorns

sugar

groundnut oil

4 Add the mushrooms and white spring onions to the wok and stir-fry for 2 minutes. Pour in the marinade mixture and stir for 1 minute until thickened.

5 Return the tofu to the wok with the green spring onions. Simmer gently for 1–2 minutes. Serve at once with rice noodles and scattered with basil leaves.

Mixed Roasted Vegetables

Frying Parmesan cheese in this unusual way gives a wonderful crusty coating to the vegetables and creates a truly Mediterranean flavour.

Serves 4 as an accompaniment

INGREDIENTS
1 large aubergine, about 225 g/8 oz
salt, for sprinkling
175 g/6 oz plum tomatoes
2 red peppers
1 yellow pepper
30 ml/2 tbsp olive oil
25 g/1 oz Parmesan cheese
30 ml/2 tbsp fresh parsley, chopped
freshly ground black pepper

peppers

plum tomatoes

aubergine

1 Cut the aubergine into segments lengthwise. Place in a colander and sprinkle with salt. Leave for 30 minutes, to allow the salt to draw out the bitter juices.

2 Rinse off the salt under cold water and pat dry on kitchen towels.

3 Cut the plum tomatoes into segments lengthwise.

4 Cut the red and yellow peppers into quarters lengthwise and deseed.

5 Heat the wok, then add 5 ml/1 tsp of the olive oil. When the oil is hot, add the Parmesan and stir-fry until golden brown. Remove from the wok, allow to cool and chop into fine flakes.

6 Heat the wok, and then add the remaining oil. When the oil is hot stir-fry the aubergine and peppers for 4–5 minutes. Stir in the tomatoes and stir-fry for a further 1 minute. Toss the vegetables in the Parmesan, parsley and black pepper and serve.

Mooli, Beetroot and Carrot Stir-fry

This is a dazzling colourful dish with a crunchy texture and fragrant taste.

Serves 4 as an accompaniment

INGREDIENTS
25 g/1 oz/¼ cup pine nuts
115 g/4 oz mooli, peeled
115 g/4 oz raw beetroot, peeled
115 g/4 oz carrots, peeled
20 ml/1½ tbsp vegetable oil
juice of 1 orange
30 ml/2 tbsp fresh coriander, chopped
salt and freshly ground black pepper

carrot

pine nuts *mooli*

beetroot

1 Heat the wok, then add the pine nuts and toss until golden brown. Remove and set aside.

2 Cut the mooli, beetroot and carrots into long thin strips.

3 Heat the wok and add one-third of the oil. When the oil is hot, stir-fry the mooli, beetroot and carrots for 2–3 minutes. Remove and set aside.

4 Pour the orange juice into the wok and simmer for 2 minutes. Remove and keep warm.

5 Arrange the vegetables in bundles, and sprinkle over the coriander and salt and pepper.

6 Drizzle over the orange juice, sprinkle in the pine nuts, and serve.

Pok Choi and Mushroom Stir-fry

Try to buy all the varieties of mushroom for this dish; the wild oyster and shitake mushrooms have particularly distinctive, delicate flavours.

Serves 4 as an accompaniment

INGREDIENTS
4 dried black Chinese mushrooms
450 g/1 lb pok choi
50 g/2 oz oyster mushrooms
50 g/2 oz shitake mushrooms
15 ml/1 tbsp vegetable oil
1 clove garlic, crushed
30 ml/2 tbsp oyster sauce

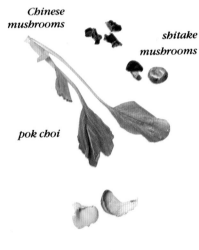

Chinese mushrooms

shitake mushrooms

pok choi

oyster mushrooms

1 Soak the black Chinese mushrooms in 150 ml/¼ pint/⅔ cup boiling water for 15 minutes to soften.

2 Tear the pok choi into bite-size pieces with your fingers.

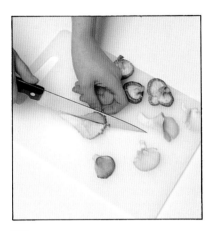

3 Halve any large oyster or shitake mushrooms, using a sharp knife.

4 Strain the Chinese mushrooms. Heat the wok, then add the oil. When the oil is hot, stir-fry the garlic until softened but not coloured.

5 Add the pok choi and stir-fry for 1 minute. Mix in all the mushrooms and stir-fry for 1 minute.

6 Add the oyster sauce, toss well and serve immediately.

Spicy Chick-Peas with Fresh Ginger

Chick-peas are filling, nourishing and cheap. Here they are served with a refreshing raita made with spring onions and mint. Serve as a snack or as part of a main meal.

Serves 4–6

INGREDIENTS
225 g/8 oz dried chick-peas
30 ml/2 tbsp vegetable oil
1 small onion, chopped
4 cm/1½ in piece fresh root
 ginger, finely chopped
2 garlic cloves, finely chopped
1.5 ml/¼ tsp ground turmeric
450 g/1 lb tomatoes, peeled,
 seeded and chopped
30 ml/2 tbsp chopped
 fresh coriander
10 ml/2 tsp garam masala
salt and pepper
fresh coriander sprigs, to garnish

FOR THE RAITA
150 ml/¼ pint/⅔ cup yogurt
2 spring onions, finely chopped
5 ml/1 tsp roasted cumin seeds
30 ml/2 tbsp chopped fresh mint
pinch of cayenne pepper,
 or to taste

VARIATION
You can replace the dried chick-peas with 2 x 425g/15oz cans chick-peas. Drain and rinse thoroughly before adding to the tomatoes in step 3.

1 Put the chick-peas in a large bowl and pour over enough cold water to cover. Leave to soak overnight. The next day, drain the chick-peas and put them in a large pan with fresh cold water to cover. Bring to the boil, then boil hard for 10 minutes. Lower the heat and simmer gently for 1½–2 hours until tender. Drain well.

2 Heat a karahi or wok until hot, add the oil and swirl it around. Add the onion and stir-fry for 2–3 minutes, then add the ginger, garlic and turmeric. Stir-fry for a few seconds more.

3 Add the tomatoes, chick-peas and seasoning, bring to the boil, then simmer for 10–15 until the tomatoes have reduced to a thick sauce.

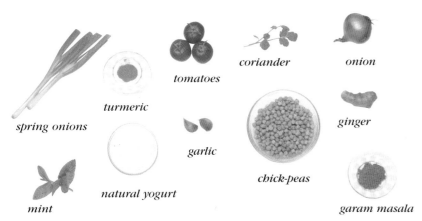

spring onions *turmeric* *tomatoes* *coriander* *onion* *garlic* *chick-peas* *ginger* *natural yogurt* *mint* *garam masala*

4 Meanwhile, make the raita: mix together the yogurt, spring onions, roasted cumin seeds, mint and cayenne pepper to taste. Set aside.

5 Just before the end of cooking, stir the chopped coriander and garam masala into the chick-peas. Serve at once, garnished with coriander sprigs and accompanied by the raita.

Beancurd Stir-fry

The beancurd has a pleasant creamy texture, which contrasts well with crunchy stir-fried vegetables. Make sure you buy firm beancurd which is easy to cut neatly.

Serves 2–4

INGREDIENTS

115 g/4 oz hard white cabbage
2 green chillies
225 g/8 oz firm beancurd
45 ml/3 tbsp vegetable oil
2 cloves garlic, crushed
3 spring onions, chopped
175 g/6 oz French beans, topped and tailed
175 g/6 oz baby sweetcorn, halved
115 g/4 oz beansprouts
45 ml/3 tbsp smooth peanut butter
20 ml/1½ tbsp dark soy sauce
300 ml/½ pint/1¼ cups coconut milk

baby sweetcorn

beansprouts

chilli

beancurd

French beans

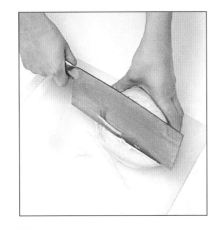

1 Shred the white cabbage. Carefully remove the seeds from the chillies and chop finely. Wear rubber gloves to protect your hands, if necessary.

2 Cut the beancurd into strips.

3 Heat the wok, then add 30 ml/2 tbsp of the oil. When the oil is hot, add the beancurd, stir-fry for 3 minutes and remove. Set aside. Wipe out the wok with kitchen towels.

4 Add the remaining oil. When it is hot, add the garlic, onions and chillies and stir-fry for 1 minute. Add the French beans, sweetcorn and beansprouts and stir-fry for a further 2 minutes.

5 Add the peanut butter and soy sauce. Stir well to coat the vegetables. Add the beancurd to the vegetables.

6 Pour the coconut milk over the vegetables, simmer for 3 minutes and serve immediately.

Black Bean and Vegetable Stir-fry

The secret of a quick stir-fry is to prepare all the ingredients first. This colourful vegetable mixture is coated in a classic Chinese sauce.

Serves 4

INGREDIENTS
8 spring onions
225 g/8 oz/2 cups button
  mushrooms
1 red pepper
1 green pepper
2 large carrots
60 ml/4 tbsp sesame oil
2 garlic cloves, crushed
60 ml/4 tbsp black bean sauce
90 ml/6 tbsp warm water
225 g/8 oz beansprouts
salt and freshly ground black pepper

1 Thinly slice the spring onions and button mushrooms.

2 Cut both the peppers in half, remove the seeds and slice the flesh into thin strips.

spring onions

black bean sauce

sesame oil

button mushrooms

red pepper

beansprouts

carrots

garlic cloves

onion

green pepper

3 Cut the carrots in half. Cut each half into thin strips lengthways. Stack the slices and cut through them to make very fine strips.

4 Heat the oil in a large wok or frying pan until very hot. Add the spring onions and garlic and stir-fry for 30 seconds.

5 Add the mushrooms, peppers and carrots. Stir-fry for 5–6 minutes over a high heat until the vegetables are just beginning to soften.

6 Mix the black bean sauce with the water. Add to the wok or pan and cook for 3–4 minutes. Stir in the beansprouts and stir-fry for 1 minute more, until all the vegetables are coated in the sauce. Season to taste. Serve at once.

COOK'S TIP
For best results the oil in the wok must be very hot before adding the vegetables.

Lentil Stir-fry

Mushrooms, artichokes, sugar snap peas and lentils make a satisfying stir-fry supper.

Serves 2–3

INGREDIENTS

115 g/4 oz sugar snap peas
25 g/1 oz butter
1 small onion, chopped
115 g/4 oz cup or brown cap
  mushrooms, sliced
400 g/14 oz can artichoke hearts,
  drained and halved
400 g/14 oz can green
  lentils, drained
60 ml/4 tbsp single cream
25 g/1 oz/¼ cup flaked
  almonds, toasted
salt and freshly ground black pepper
French bread, to serve

single cream   *green lentils*

cup mushrooms

sugar snap peas

flaked almonds

artichoke hearts

onion

COOK'S TIP

Use Greek yogurt instead of the cream, if preferred.

1 Bring a pan of salted water to the boil, add the sugar snap peas and cook for about 4 minutes until just tender. Drain, refresh under cold running water, then drain again. Pat dry the peas with kitchen paper and set aside.

2 Melt the butter in a frying pan. Cook the chopped onion for 2–3 minutes, stirring occasionally.

3 Add the sliced mushrooms to the onion. Stir until combined, then cook for 2–3 minutes until just tender. Add the artichokes, sugar snap peas and lentils to the pan. Stir-fry for 2 minutes.

4 Stir in the cream and almonds and cook for 1 minute. Season to taste. Serve at once, with chunks of French bread.

Vegetable Fajita

A colourful medley of mushrooms and peppers in a spicy sauce, wrapped in tortillas and served with creamy guacamole.

Serves 2

INGREDIENTS
1 onion
1 red pepper
1 green pepper
1 yellow pepper
·1 garlic clove, crushed
225 g/8 oz mushrooms
90 ml/6 tbsp vegetable oil
30 ml/2 tbsp medium chilli powder
salt and freshly ground black pepper
coriander sprigs and 1 lime, cut into
   wedges, to garnish

FOR THE GUACAMOLE
1 ripe avocado
1 shallot, roughly chopped
1 green chilli, seeded and
   roughly chopped
juice of 1 lime

TO SERVE
4–6 flour tortillas, warmed

green pepper *yellow pepper* *red pepper*

mushrooms *green chilli*

garlic clove

shallot

avocado

lime *chilli powder* *onion*

1 Slice the onion. Cut the peppers in half, remove the seeds and cut the flesh into strips. Combine the onion and peppers in a bowl. Add the crushed garlic and mix lightly.

2 Remove the mushroom stalks. Save for making stock, or discard. Slice the mushroom caps and add to the pepper mixture in the bowl. Mix the oil and chilli powder in a cup, pour over the vegetable mixture and stir well. Set aside.

3 Make the guacamole. Cut the avocado in half and remove the stone and the peel. Put the flesh into a food processor or blender with the shallot, green chilli and lime juice. Process for 1 minute until smooth. Scrape into a small bowl, cover closely and put in the fridge to chill until required.

4 Heat a frying pan or wok until very hot. Add the marinated vegetables and stir-fry over high heat for 5–6 minutes until the mushrooms and pepper are just tender. Season well. Spoon a little of the filling on to each tortilla and roll up. Garnish with fresh coriander and lime wedges and serve with the guacamole.

Crispy Noodles with Mixed Vegetables

In this dish, rice vermicelli noodles are deep-fried until crisp, then tossed into a colourful selection of stir-fried vegetables.

COOK'S TIP
If a milder flavour is preferred, remove the seeds from the chilli.

Serves 3–4

INGREDIENTS
2 large carrots
2 courgettes
4 spring onions
115 g/4 oz yard-long beans or green beans
115 g/4 oz dried vermicelli rice noodles or cellophane noodles
groundnut oil, for deep frying
2.5 cm/1 in piece fresh root ginger, cut into shreds
1 fresh red chilli, sliced
115 g/4 oz fresh shiitake or button mushrooms, thickly sliced
few Chinese cabbage leaves, coarsely shredded
75 g/3 oz beansprouts
30 ml/2 tbsp light soy sauce
30 ml/2 tbsp Chinese rice wine
5 ml/1 tsp sugar
30 ml/2 tbsp roughly torn coriander leaves

spring onions *mushrooms* *coriander* *yard-long beans* *red chillies* *carrot* *Chinese cabbage* *beansprouts* *courgettes* *ginger* *Chinese rice wine* *light soy sauce*

1 Cut the carrots and courgettes into fine sticks. Shred the spring onions into similar-size pieces. Trim the beans. If using yard-long beans, cut them into short lengths.

2 Break the noodles into lengths of about 7.5 cm/3 in. Half-fill a wok with oil and heat it to 180°C/350°F. Deep fry the raw noodles, a handful at a time, for 1–2 minutes until puffed and crispy. Drain on kitchen paper. Carefully pour off all but 30 ml/2 tbsp of the oil.

3 Reheat the oil in the wok. When hot, add the beans and stir-fry for 2–3 minutes. Add the ginger, red chilli, mushrooms, carrots and courgettes and stir-fry for 1–2 minutes.

4 Add the Chinese cabbage, beansprouts and spring onions. Stir-fry for 1 minute, then add the soy sauce, rice wine and sugar. Cook, stirring, for about 30 seconds.

5 Add the noodles and coriander and toss to mix, taking care not to crush the noodles too much. Serve at once, piled up on a plate.

Nasi Goreng

This dish is originally from Thailand, but can easily be adapted by adding any cooked ingredients you have to hand. Crispy prawn crackers make an ideal accompaniment.

Serves 4

INGREDIENTS
225 g/8 oz long grain rice
2 × size 3 eggs
30 ml/2 tbsp vegetable oil
1 green chilli
2 spring onions, roughly chopped
2 cloves garlic, crushed
225 g/8 oz cooked chicken
225 g/8 oz cooked prawns
45 ml/3 tbsp dark soy sauce
prawn crackers, to serve

rice

soy sauce

egg

chilli

prawns

1 Rinse the rice and then cook for 10–12 minutes in 500 ml/1 pint water in a saucepan with a tight-fitting lid. When cooked, refresh under cold water.

2 Lightly beat the eggs. Heat 15 ml/ 1 tbsp of oil in a small frying pan and swirl in the beaten egg. When cooked on one side, flip over and cook on the other side, remove from the pan and leave to cool. Cut the omelette into strips.

3 Carefully remove the seeds from the chilli and chop finely, wearing rubber gloves to protect your hands if necessary. Place the spring onions, chilli and garlic in a food processor and blend to a paste.

4 Heat the wok, and then add the remaining oil. When the oil is hot, add the paste and stir-fry for 1 minute.

5 Add the chicken and prawns.

6 Add the rice and stir-fry for 3–4 minutes. Stir in the soy sauce and serve with prawn crackers.

Thai Fried Rice

This hot and spicy dish is easy to prepare and makes a meal in itself.

Serves 4

INGREDIENTS
225 g/8 oz Thai jasmine rice
45 ml/3 tbsp vegetable oil
1 onion, chopped
1 small red pepper, seeded and
　cut into 2 cm/¾ in cubes
350 g/12 oz skinless and boneless
　chicken breasts, cut into 2 cm/
　¾ in cubes
1 garlic clove, crushed
15 ml/1 tbsp mild curry paste
2.5 ml/½ tsp paprika
2.5 ml/½ tsp ground turmeric
30 ml/2 tbsp Thai fish sauce
　(*nam pla*)
2 eggs, beaten
salt and ground black pepper
fried basil leaves, to garnish

rice

Thai fish sauce

chicken

curry paste

onion

egg

red pepper

turmeric

paprika

vegetable oil

VARIATION
Add 50 g/2 oz frozen peas to the chicken in step 3, if you wish.

1 Put the rice in a sieve and wash well under cold running water. Put the rice in a heavy-based pan with 1.5 litres/2½ pints/6¼ cups boiling water. Return to the boil, then simmer, uncovered, for 8–10 minutes; drain well. Spread out the grains on a tray and leave to cool.

2 Heat a wok until hot, add 30ml/ 2 tbsp of the oil and swirl it around. Add the onion and red pepper and stir-fry for 1 minute.

3 Add the chicken, garlic, curry paste and spices and stir-fry for 2–3 minutes.

4 Reduce the heat to medium, add the cooled rice, fish sauce and seasoning. Stir-fry for 2–3 minutes until the rice is very hot.

5 Make a well in the centre of the rice and add the remaining oil. When hot, add the beaten eggs, leave to cook for about 2 minutes until lightly set, then stir into the rice.

6 Scatter over the fried basil leaves and serve at once.

Stir-fried Noodles with Sweet Soy Salmon

Teriyaki sauce forms the marinade for the salmon in this recipe. Served with soft-fried noodles, it makes a stunning dish.

COOK'S TIP
It is important to scrape the marinade off the fish as any remaining pieces of ginger or garlic would burn during grilling and spoil the finished dish.

Serves 4

INGREDIENTS
350 g/12 oz salmon fillet
30 ml/2 tbsp Japanese soy
  sauce (*shoyu*)
30 ml/2 tbsp sake
60 ml/4 tbsp mirin or
  sweet sherry
5 ml/1 tsp light brown soft sugar
10 ml/2 tsp grated fresh
  root ginger
3 garlic cloves, 1 crushed, and
  2 sliced into rounds
30 ml/2 tbsp groundnut oil
225 g/8 oz dried egg noodles,
  cooked and drained
50 g/2 oz alfalfa sprouts
30 ml/2 tbsp sesame seeds,
  lightly toasted

garlic
sesame seeds
noodles
alfalfa sprouts
sake
mirin
sugar
salmon
Japanese soy sauce
groundnut oil
ginger

1 Thinly slice the salmon, then place in a shallow dish.

2 In a bowl, mix together the soy sauce, sake, mirin or sherry, sugar, ginger and crushed garlic. Pour over the salmon, cover and leave for 30 minutes.

3 Preheat the grill. Drain the salmon, scraping off and reserving the marinade. Place the salmon in a single layer on a baking sheet. Cook under the grill for 2–3 minutes without turning.

4 Meanwhile, heat a wok until hot, add the oil and swirl it around. Add the garlic rounds and cook until golden brown but not burnt.

5 Add the cooked noodles and reserved marinade to the wok and stir-fry for 3–4 minutes until the marinade has reduced slightly to a syrupy glaze and coats the noodles.

6 Toss in the alfalfa sprouts, then remove immediately from the heat. Transfer to warmed serving plates and top with the salmon. Sprinkle over the toasted sesame seeds. Serve at once.

Nutty Rice and Mushroom Stir-fry

This delicious and substantial supper dish can be eaten hot or cold with salads.

Serves 4–6

INGREDIENTS
350 g/12 oz long grain rice
45 ml/3 tbsp sunflower oil
1 small onion, roughly chopped
225 g/8 oz field mushrooms, sliced
50 g/2 oz/½ cup hazelnuts,
   roughly chopped
50 g/2 oz/½ cup pecan nuts,
   roughly chopped
50 g/2 oz/½ cup almonds,
   roughly chopped
60 ml/4 tbsp fresh parsley, chopped
salt and freshly ground black pepper

rice

almonds

field mushroom

hazelnuts

pecan nuts

1 Rinse the rice, then cook for 10–12 minutes in 700–850 ml/1¼–1½ pints water in a saucepan with a tight-fitting lid. When cooked, refresh under cold water. Heat the wok, then add half the oil. When the oil is hot, stir-fry the rice for 2–3 minutes. Remove and set aside.

2 Add the remaining oil and stir-fry the onion for 2 minutes until softened.

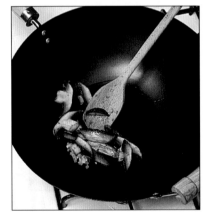

3 Mix in the field mushrooms and stir-fry for 2 minutes.

4 Add all the nuts and stir-fry for 1 minute. Return the rice to the wok and stir-fry for 3 minutes. Season with salt and pepper. Stir in the parsley and serve.

Mee Krob

This delicious dish makes a filling meal. Take care when frying vermicelli as it has a tendency to spit when added to hot oil.

Serves 4

INGREDIENTS

125 ml/4 fl oz/½ cup vegetable oil
225 g/8 oz rice vermicelli
150 g/5 oz French beans, topped,
    tailed and halved lengthwise
1 onion, finely chopped
2 boneless, skinless chicken breasts,
    about 175 g/6 oz each, cut
    into strips
5 ml/1 tsp chilli powder
225 g/8 oz cooked prawns
45 ml/3 tbsp dark soy sauce
45 ml/3 tbsp white wine vinegar
10 ml/2 tsp caster sugar
fresh coriander sprigs, to garnish

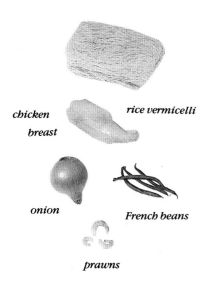

chicken breast

rice vermicelli

onion

French beans

prawns

1 Heat the wok, then add 60 ml/4 tbsp of the oil. Break up the vermicelli into 7.5 cm/3 in lengths. When the oil is hot, fry the vermicelli in batches. Remove from the heat and keep warm.

2 Heat the remaining oil in the wok, then add the French beans, onion and chicken and stir-fry for 3 minutes until the chicken is cooked.

3 Sprinkle in the chilli powder. Stir in the prawns, soy sauce, vinegar and sugar, and stir-fry for 2 minutes.

4 Serve the chicken, prawns and vegetables on the vermicelli, garnished with sprigs of fresh coriander.

Fried Singapore Noodles

Thai fish cakes vary in their size, and their hotness. You can buy them from Oriental supermarkets, but, if you cannot get hold of them, simply omit them from the recipe.

Serves 4

INGREDIENTS
175 g/6 oz rice noodles
60 ml/4 tbsp vegetable oil
2.5 ml/½ tsp salt
75 g/3 oz cooked prawns
175 g/6 oz cooked pork, cut
　　into matchsticks
1 green pepper, seeded and chopped
　　into matchsticks
2.5 ml/½ tsp sugar
10 ml/2 tsp curry powder
75 g/3 oz Thai fish cakes
10 ml/2 tsp dark soy sauce

rice noodles

pork

pepper

prawns

1 Soak the rice noodles in water for about 10 minutes, drain well, then pat dry with kitchen towels.

2 Heat the wok, then add half the oil. When the oil is hot, add the noodles and salt and stir-fry for 2 minutes. Transfer to a heated serving dish to keep warm.

3 Heat the remaining oil and add the prawns, pork, pepper, sugar, curry powder and remaining salt. Stir-fry the ingredients for 1 minute.

4 Return the noodles to the pan and stir-fry with the Thai fish cakes for 2 minutes. Stir in the soy sauce and serve

Oriental Vegetable Noodles

Thin Italian egg pasta is a good alternative to Oriental egg noodles; use it fresh or dried.

Serves 6

INGREDIENTS

500 g/1¼ lb thin tagliarini
1 red onion
115 g/4 oz shitake mushrooms
45 ml/3 tbsp sesame oil
45 ml/3 tbsp dark soy sauce
15 ml/1 tbsp balsamic vinegar
10 ml/2 tsp caster sugar
5 ml/1 tsp salt
celery leaves, to garnish

tagliarini

shitake mushrooms

red onion

balsamic vinegar

soy sauce

1 Boil the tagliarini in a large pan of salted boiling water, following the instructions on the pack.

2 Thinly slice the red onion and the mushrooms, using a sharp knife.

3 Heat the wok, then add 15 ml/1 tbsp of the sesame oil. When the oil is hot, stir-fry the onion and mushrooms for 2 minutes.

4 Drain the tagliarini, then add to the wok with the soy sauce, balsamic vinegar, sugar and salt. Stir-fry for 1 minute, then add the remaining sesame oil, and serve garnished with celery leaves.

Chinese Jewelled Rice

This rice dish, with its many different, interesting ingredients, can make a meal in itself.

Serves 4

INGREDIENTS
350 g/12 oz long grain rice
45 ml/3 tbsp vegetable oil
1 onion, roughly chopped
115 g/4 oz cooked ham, diced
175 g/6 oz canned white crabmeat
75 g/3 oz canned water chestnuts, drained and cut into cubes
4 dried black Chinese mushrooms, soaked, drained and cut into dice
115 g/4 oz peas, thawed if frozen
30 ml/2 tbsp oyster sauce
5 ml/1 tsp sugar

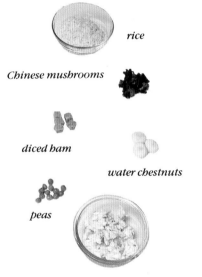

rice

Chinese mushrooms

diced ham

water chestnuts

peas

crabmeat

1 Rinse the rice, then cook for 10–12 minutes in 700–850 ml/1 1/4–1 1/2 pints water in a saucepan with a tight-fitting lid. When cooked, refresh under cold water. Heat the wok, then add half the oil. When the oil is hot, stir-fry the rice for 3 minutes, then remove and set aside.

2 Add the remaining oil to the wok. When the oil is hot, cook the onion until softened but not coloured.

3 Add all the remaining ingredients and stir-fry for 2 minutes.

4 Return the rice to the wok and stir-fry for 3 minutes, then serve.

Mixed Rice Noodles

A delicious noodle dish made extra special by adding avocado and garnishing with prawns.

Serves 4

INGREDIENTS
15 ml/1 tbsp sunflower oil
2.5 cm/1 in piece root ginger, peeled and grated
2 cloves garlic, crushed
45 ml/3 tbsp dark soy sauce
225 g/8 oz peas, thawed if frozen
450 g/1 lb rice noodles
450 g/1 lb fresh spinach, coarse stalks removed
30 ml/2 tbsp smooth peanut butter
30 ml/2 tbsp tahini
150 ml/¼ pint/⅔ cup milk
1 ripe avocado, peeled and stoned
roasted peanuts and peeled prawns, to garnish

rice noodles

ginger

peas

peanut butter

spinach

1 Heat the wok, then add the oil. When the oil is hot, stir-fry the ginger and garlic for 30 seconds. Add 15 ml/1 tbsp of the soy sauce and 150 ml/¼ pint/⅔ cup boiling water.

2 Add the peas and noodles, then cook for 3 minutes. Stir in the spinach. Remove the vegetables and noodles, drain and keep warm.

3 Stir the peanut butter, remaining soy sauce, tahini and milk together in the wok, and simmer for 1 minute.

4 Add the vegetables and noodles, slice in the avocado and toss together. Serve piled on individual plates. Spoon some sauce over each portion and garnish with peanuts and prawns.

Spicy Fried Rice Sticks with Prawns

This recipe is based on the classic Thai noodle dish called *Pad Thai*. Popular all over Thailand, it is enjoyed morning, noon and night.

VARIATION
For a vegetarian dish omit the dried shrimps and replace the king prawns with cubes of deep-fried tofu.

Serves 4

INGREDIENTS
15 g/½ oz dried shrimps
15 ml/1 tbsp tamarind pulp
45 ml/3 tbsp Thai fish sauce
   (*nam pla*)
15 ml/1 tbsp sugar
2 garlic cloves, chopped
2 fresh red chillies, seeded and
   chopped
45 ml/3 tbsp groundnut oil
2 eggs, beaten
225 g/8 oz dried rice sticks,
   soaked in warm water for
   30 minutes, refreshed under
   cold running water and drained
225 g/8 oz cooked peeled
   king prawns
3 spring onions, cut into
   2.5 cm/1 in lengths
75 g/3 oz beansprouts
30 ml/2 tbsp roughly chopped
   roasted unsalted peanuts
30 ml/2 tbsp chopped
   fresh coriander
lime slices, to garnish

1 Put the dried shrimps in a small bowl and pour over enough warm water to cover. Leave to soak for 30 minutes until soft; drain.

2 Put the tamarind pulp in a bowl with 60 ml/4 tbsp hot water. Blend together, then press through a sieve to extract 30 ml/2 tbsp thick tamarind water. Mix the tamarind water with the fish sauce and sugar.

3 Using a mortar and pestle, pound the garlic and chillies to form a paste. Heat a wok over a medium heat, add 15 ml/1 tbsp of the oil, then add the beaten eggs and stir for 1–2 minutes until the eggs are scrambled. Remove and set aside. Wipe the wok clean.

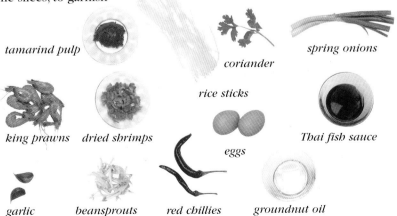

tamarind pulp

coriander

spring onions

rice sticks

king prawns   *dried shrimps*

eggs

Thai fish sauce

garlic   *beansprouts*   *red chillies*   *groundnut oil*

4 Reheat the wok until hot, add the remaining oil, then the chilli paste and dried shrimps and stir-fry for 1 minute. Add the rice sticks and tamarind mixture and stir-fry for 3–4 minutes.

5 Add the scrambled eggs, prawns, spring onions, beansprouts, peanuts and coriander, then stir-fry for 2 minutes until well mixed. Serve at once, garnishing each portion with lime slices.

Fried Rice with Spices

This dish is mildly spiced, suitable as an accompaniment to any curried dish. The whole spices are not meant to be eaten.

Serves 3-4

INGREDIENTS
175 g/6 oz/1¼ cups basmati rice
2.5 ml/½ tsp salt
15 ml/1 tbsp ghee or butter
8 whole cloves
4 green cardamom pods, bruised
1 bay leaf
7.5 cm/3 in cinnamon stick
5 ml/1 tsp black peppercorns
5 ml/1 tsp cumin seeds
5 ml/1 tsp coriander seeds

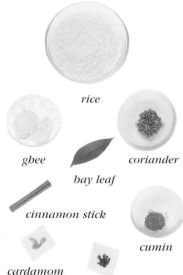

rice

ghee   *coriander*

bay leaf

cinnamon stick

cumin

cardamom

cloves

VARIATION
You could add 2.5 ml/½ tsp ground turmeric to the rice in step 2 to colour it yellow.

1 Put the rice in a colander and wash under cold running water until the water clears. Put in a bowl and pour 600 ml/ 1 pint/2½ cups fresh water over the rice. Leave the rice to soak for 30 minutes; then drain thoroughly.

2 Put the rice, salt and 600ml/ 1 pint/2½ cups water in a heavy-based pan. Bring to the boil, then simmer, covered, for about 10 minutes. The rice should be just cooked with still a little bite to it. Drain off any excess water, fluff up the grains with a fork, then spread it out on a tray and leave to cool.

3 Heat the ghee or butter in a karahi or wok until foaming, add the spices and stir-fry for 1 minute.

4 Add the cooled rice and stir-fry for 3–4 minutes until warmed through. Serve at once.

Singapore Noodles

A delicious supper dish with a stunning mix of flavours and textures.

Serves 4

INGREDIENTS

225 g/8 oz dried egg noodles
45 ml/3 tbsp groundnut oil
1 onion, chopped
2.5 cm/1 in piece fresh root
  ginger, finely chopped
1 garlic clove, finely chopped
15 ml/1 tbsp Madras
  curry powder
2.5 ml/½ tsp salt
115 g/4 oz cooked chicken or
  pork, finely shredded
115 g/4 oz cooked peeled prawns
115 g/4 oz Chinese cabbage
  leaves, shredded
115 g/4 oz beansprouts
60 ml/4 tbsp chicken stock
15–30 ml/1–2 tbsp dark soy sauce
1–2 fresh red chillies, seeded
  and finely shredded
4 spring onions, finely shredded

beansprouts

noodles

Chinese cabbage

ginger

curry powder

chicken

dark soy sauce

onion

stock

red chillies

spring onions

groundnut oil

prawns

1 Cook the noodles according to the packet instructions. Rinse thoroughly under cold water and drain well. Toss in 15 ml/1 tbsp of the oil and set aside.

2 Heat a wok until hot, add the remaining oil and swirl it around. Add the onion, ginger and garlic and stir-fry for about 2 minutes.

3 Add the curry powder and salt, stir-fry for 30 seconds, then add the egg noodles, chicken or pork and prawns. Stir-fry for 3–4 minutes.

4 Add the Chinese cabbage and beansprouts and stir-fry for 1–2 minutes. Sprinkle in the stock and soy sauce to taste and toss well until evenly mixed. Serve at once, garnished with the shredded red chillies and spring onions.

Indonesian Fried Rice

This fried rice dish makes an ideal supper on its own or as an accompaniment.

Serves 4-6

INGREDIENTS
4 shallots, roughly chopped
1 fresh red chilli, seeded
   and chopped
1 garlic clove, chopped
thin sliver of dried shrimp paste
45 ml/3 tbsp vegetable oil
225 g/8 oz boneless lean pork,
   cut into fine strips
175 g/6 oz/1¼ cups long grain
   white rice, boiled and cooled
3-4 spring onions, thinly sliced
115 g/4 oz cooked peeled prawns
30 ml/2 tbsp sweet soy sauce
   (*kecap manis*)
chopped fresh coriander and
   fine cucumber shreds, to
   garnish

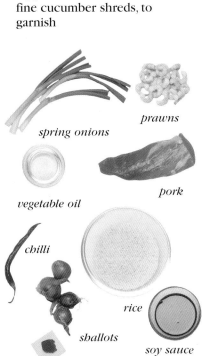

spring onions

prawns

vegetable oil

pork

chilli

rice

shallots

soy sauce

dried shrimp paste

garlic

1 In a mortar pound the shallots, chilli, garlic and shrimp paste with a pestle until they form a paste.

2 Heat a wok until hot, add 30 ml/ 2 tbsp of the oil and swirl it around. Add the pork and stir-fry for 2–3 minutes. Remove the pork from the wok, set aside and keep warm.

3 Add the remaining oil to the wok. When hot, add the spiced shallot paste and stir-fry for about 30 seconds.

4 Reduce the heat. Add the rice, spring onions and prawns. Stir-fry for 2–3 minutes. Add the pork and sprinkle over the soy sauce. Stir-fry for 1 minute. Serve garnished with the chopped coriander and cucumber shreds.

Noodles with Ginger and Coriander

Here is a simple noodle dish that goes well with most oriental dishes. It can also be served as a snack for 2-3 people.

Serves 4-6

INGREDIENTS
handful of fresh coriander sprigs
225 g/8 oz dried egg noodles
45 ml/3 tbsp groundnut oil
5 cm/2 in piece fresh root ginger, cut into fine shreds
6-8 spring onions, cut into shreds
30 ml/2 tbsp light soy sauce
salt and ground black pepper

spring onions

groundnut oil

ginger

coriander

noodles

light soy sauce

COOK'S TIP

Many of the dried egg noodles available are sold packed in layers. As a guide allow 1 layer of noodles per person as an average portion for a main dish.

1 Strip the leaves from the coriander stalks. Pile them on a chopping board and coarsely chop them using a cleaver or large sharp knife.

2 Cook the noodles according to the packet instructions. Rinse under cold water and drain well. Toss in 15 ml/ 1 tbsp of the oil.

3 Heat a wok until hot, add the remaining oil and swirl it around. Add the ginger and stir-fry for a few seconds, then add the noodles and spring onions. Stir-fry for 3–4 minutes until hot.

4 Sprinkle over the soy sauce, coriander and seasoning. Toss well, then serve at once.

Stir-fried Tofu and Beansprouts with Noodles

This is a satisfying dish, which is both tasty and easy to make.

Serves 4

INGREDIENTS
225 g/8 oz firm tofu
groundnut oil, for deep frying
175 g/6 oz medium egg noodles
15 ml/1 tbsp sesame oil
5 ml/1 tsp cornflour
10 ml/2 tsp dark soy sauce
30 ml/1 tbsp Chinese rice wine
5 ml/1 tsp sugar
6–8 spring onions, cut diagonally
    into 2.5 cm/1 in lengths
3 garlic cloves, sliced
1 fresh green chilli, seeded
    and sliced
115 g/4 oz Chinese cabbage
    leaves, coarsely shredded
50 g/2 oz beansprouts
50 g/2 oz cashew nuts, toasted

spring onion

garlic

sesame oil

Chinese cabbage

tofu

noodles

beansprouts

dark soy sauce

Chinese rice wine

green chilli

1 Drain the tofu and pat dry with kitchen paper. Cut the tofu into 2.5 cm/ 1 in cubes. Half-fill a wok with groundnut oil and heat to 180°C/350°F. Deep-fry the tofu in batches for 1–2 minutes until golden and crisp. Drain on kitchen paper. Carefully pour all but 30 ml/2 tbsp of the oil from the wok.

2 Cook the noodles. Rinse them thoroughly under cold water and drain well. Toss in 10 ml/2 tsp of the sesame oil and set aside. In a bowl, blend together the cornflour, soy sauce, rice wine, sugar and remaining sesame oil.

3 Reheat the 30 ml/2 tbsp of groundnut oil and, when hot, add the spring onions, garlic, chilli, Chinese cabbage and beansprouts. Stir-fry for 1–2 minutes.

4 Add the tofu with the noodles and sauce. Cook, stirring, for about 1 minute until well mixed. Sprinkle over the cashew nuts. Serve at once.

Chow Mein

One of the most well-known Chinese dishes, this recipe is both easy to prepare and healthy.

Serves 4

INGREDIENTS
225 g/8 oz dried egg noodles
30 ml/2 tbsp oil
1 onion, chopped
1.25 cm/½ in fresh root ginger, chopped
2 garlic cloves, crushed
30 ml/2 tbsp soy sauce
60 ml/2 fl oz/¼ cup dry white wine
10 ml/2 tsp Chinese five-spice powder
450 g/1 lb/4 cups minced pork
4 spring onions, sliced
50 g/2 oz oyster mushrooms
75 g/3 oz bamboo shoots
15 ml/1 tbsp sesame oil
prawn crackers, to serve

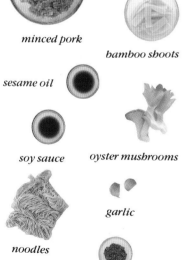

minced pork

bamboo shoots

sesame oil

soy sauce   *oyster mushrooms*

noodles

garlic

five-spice powder

ginger   *onion*   *spring onions*

I Cook the noodles in boiling water for 4 minutes and drain.

2 Meanwhile, heat the oil in a wok and add the onion, ginger, garlic, soy sauce and wine. Cook for 1 minute. Stir in the Chinese five-spice powder.

3 Add the pork and cook for 10 minutes, stirring continuously. Add the spring onions, mushrooms, bamboo shoots and continue to cook for a further 5 minutes.

4 Stir in the noodles and sesame oil. Mix all the ingredients together well and serve with prawn crackers.

Red Fried Rice

This vibrant rice dish owes its appeal as much to the bright colours of red onion, red pepper and cherry tomatoes as it does to their distinctive flavours.

Serves 2

INGREDIENTS
115 g/4 oz/³/₄ cup basmati rice
30 ml/2 tbsp groundnut oil
1 small red onion, chopped
1 red pepper, seeded and chopped
225 g/8 oz cherry tomatoes, halved
2 eggs, beaten
salt and freshly ground black pepper

eggs

basmati rice

cherry tomatoes

red onion

red pepper

1 Wash the rice several times under cold running water. Drain well. Bring a large pan of water to the boil, add the rice and cook for 10–12 minutes.

2 Meanwhile, heat the oil in a wok until very hot. Add the onion and red pepper and stir-fry for 2–3 minutes. Add the cherry tomatoes and stir-fry for a further 2 minutes.

3 Pour in the beaten eggs all at once. Cook for 30 seconds without stirring, then stir to break up the egg as it sets.

4 Drain the cooked rice thoroughly, add to the wok and toss it over the heat with the vegetable and egg mixture for 3 minutes. Season the fried rice with salt and pepper to taste.

Fried Noodles with Beansprouts and Asparagus

Soft fried noodles contrast beautifully with crisp beansprouts and asparagus.

Serves 2

INGREDIENTS
115 g/4 oz dried egg noodles
60 ml/4 tbsp vegetable oil
1 small onion, chopped
2.5 cm/1 in piece of fresh root
  ginger, peeled and grated
2 garlic cloves, crushed
175 g/6 oz young asparagus
  spears, trimmed
115 g/4 oz beansprouts
4 spring onions, sliced
45 ml/3 tbsp soy sauce
salt and freshly ground black pepper

onion

spring onions

garlic cloves

root ginger

soy sauce

egg noodles

beansprouts

asparagus spears

1 Bring a pan of salted water to the boil. Add the noodles and cook for 2–3 minutes, until just tender. Drain and toss in 30 ml/2 tbsp of the oil.

2 Heat the remaining oil in a wok or frying pan until very hot. Add the onion, ginger and garlic and stir-fry for 2–3 minutes. Add the asparagus and stir-fry for a further 2–3 minutes.

3 Add the noodles and beansprouts and stir-fry for 2 minutes.

4 Stir in the spring onions and soy sauce. Season to taste, adding salt sparingly as the soy sauce will add quite a salty flavour. Stir-fry for 1 minute, then serve at once.

Five-spice Vegetable Noodles

Vary this vegetable stir-fry by substituting mushrooms, bamboo shoots, beansprouts, mange-touts or water chestnuts for some or all of the vegetables suggested below.

Serves 2–3

INGREDIENTS
225 g/8 oz dried egg noodles
30 ml/2 tbsp sesame oil
2 carrots
1 celery stick
1 small fennel bulb
2 courgettes, halved and sliced
1 red chilli, seeded and chopped
2.5 cm/1 in piece of fresh root
  ginger, peeled and grated
1 garlic clove, crushed
7.5 ml/1½ tsp Chinese five-spice
  powder
2.5 ml/½ tsp ground cinnamon
4 spring onions, sliced
50 ml/2 fl oz/¼ cup warm water

carrots
celery stick
garlic clove
fennel bulb
egg noodles
courgettes
five-spice powder
spring onions
cinnamon
root ginger

1 Bring a large pan of salted water to the boil. Add the noodles and cook for 2–3 minutes until just tender. Drain the noodles, return them to the pan and toss in a little of the oil. Set aside.

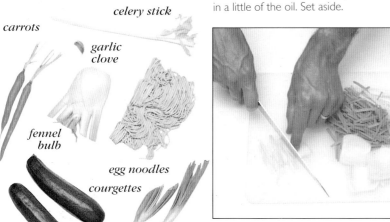

2 Cut the carrot and celery into julienne. Cut the fennel bulb in half and cut out the hard core. Cut into slices, then cut the slices into julienne.

3 Heat the remaining oil in a wok or frying pan until very hot. Add all the vegetables, including the chilli, and stir-fry for 7–8 minutes.

4 Add the ginger and garlic and stir-fry for 2 minutes, then add the spices. Cook for 1 minute. Add the spring onions and stir-fry for 1 minute. Pour in the warm water and cook for 1 minute. Stir in the noodles and toss well together. Serve sprinkled with sliced red chilli, if liked.

Stir-fried Vegetables with Pasta

This is a colourful Chinese-style dish, easily prepared using pasta instead of Chinese noodles.

Serves 4

INGREDIENTS
1 medium carrot
175 g/6 oz small courgettes (zucchini)
175 g/6 oz runner or other green beans
175 g/6 oz baby sweetcorn
450 g/1 lb ribbon pasta such as tagliatelle
salt
30 ml/2 tbsp corn oil, plus extra for tossing the pasta
1 cm/½ in piece fresh root ginger, peeled and finely chopped
2 garlic cloves, finely chopped
90 ml/6 tbsp yellow bean sauce
6 spring onions (scallions), sliced into 2.5 cm/1 in lengths
30 ml/2 tbsp dry sherry
5 ml/1 tsp sesame seeds

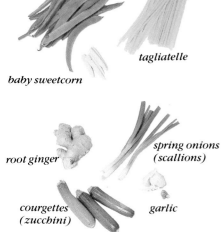

green beans

tagliatelle

baby sweetcorn

root ginger

spring onions (scallions)

courgettes (zucchini)

garlic

1 Slice the carrot and courgettes (zucchini) diagonally into chunks. Slice the beans diagonally. Cut the baby corn diagonally in half.

2 Cook the pasta in plenty of boiling salted water according to the manufacturer's instructions, drain, then rinse under hot water. Toss in a little oil.

3 Heat 30 ml/2 tbsp oil until smoking in a wok or frying pan (skillet) and add the ginger and garlic. Stir-fry for 30 seconds, then add the carrots, beans and courgettes.

4 Stir-fry for 3–4 minutes, then stir in the yellow bean sauce. Stir-fry for 2 minutes, add the spring onions (scallions), sherry and pasta and stir-fry for a further 1 minute until piping hot. Sprinkle with sesame seeds and serve immediately.

Mango and Coconut Stir-fry

Choose a ripe mango for this recipe. If you buy one that is a little under-ripe, leave it in a warm place for a day or two before using.

Serves 4

INGREDIENTS
¼ coconut
1 large, ripe mango
juice of 2 limes
rind of 2 limes, finely grated
15 ml/1 tbsp sunflower oil
15 g/½ oz/1 tbsp butter
30 ml/1½ tbsp clear honey
crème fraîche, to serve

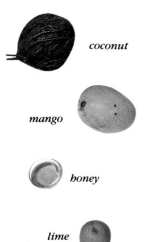

coconut

mango

honey

lime

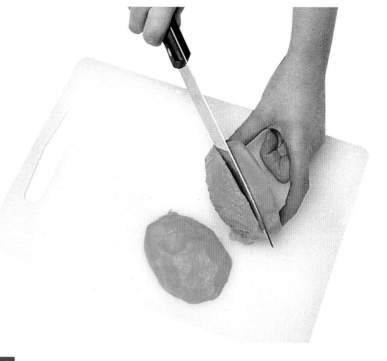

1 Prepare the coconut flakes by draining the milk from the coconut and peeling the flesh with a vegetable peeler.

2 Peel the mango. Cut the stone out of the middle of the fruit. Cut each half of the mango into slices.

COOK'S TIP

Because of the delicate taste of desserts, always make sure your wok has been scrupulously cleaned so there is no transference of flavours – a garlicky mango isn't quite the effect you want to achieve!

3 Place the mango slices in a bowl and pour over the lime juice and rind, to marinate them.

4 Meanwhile, heat the wok, then add 10 ml/2 tsp of the oil. When the oil is hot, add the butter. When the butter has melted, stir in the coconut flakes and stir-fry for 1–2 minutes until the coconut is golden brown. Remove and drain on kitchen towels. Wipe out the wok. Strain the mango slices, reserving the juice.

5 Heat the wok and add the remaining oil. When the oil is hot, add the mango and stir-fry for 1–2 minutes, then add the juice and allow to bubble and reduce for 1 minute. Then stir in the honey, sprinkle on the coconut flakes and serve with crème fraîche.

Caramelized Apples

A sweet, sticky dessert which is very quickly made,
and usually very quickly eaten!

Serves 4

INGREDIENTS
675 g/1½ lb dessert apples
115 g/4 oz/½ cup unsalted butter
25 g/1 oz fresh white breadcrumbs
50 g/2 oz/½ cup ground almonds
rind of 2 lemons, finely grated
60 ml/4 tbsp golden syrup
60 ml/4 tbsp thick Greek yogurt,
   to serve

lemon

golden syrup

ground almonds

apple

1 Peel and core the apples.

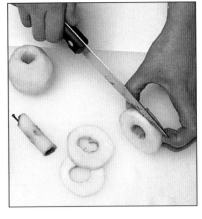

2 Carefully cut the apples into 1 cm/½ in-thick rings.

3 Heat the wok, then add the butter. When the butter has melted, add the apple rings and stir-fry for 4 minutes until golden and tender. Remove from the wok, reserving the butter. Add the breadcrumbs to the hot butter and stir-fry for 1 minute.

4 Stir in the ground almonds and lemon rind and stir-fry for a further 3 minutes, stirring constantly. Sprinkle the breadcrumb mix over the apples, then drizzle warmed golden syrup over the top. Serve with thick Greek yogurt.

Crispy Cinnamon Toasts

This recipe is based on a sweet version of French toast. You can use fancy cutters to create a pretty dessert or, if you do not have cutters, simply cut the crusts off the bread and cut it into little fingers.

Serves 4

INGREDIENTS
50 g/2 oz raisins
45 ml/3 tbsp Grand Marnier
4 medium slices white bread
3 × size 4 eggs, beaten
15 ml/1 tbsp ground cinnamon
2 large oranges
20 ml/1½ tbsp sunflower oil
25 g/1 oz/2 tbsp unsalted butter
15 ml/1 tbsp demerara sugar
thick Greek yogurt, to serve

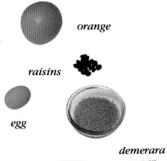

orange

raisins

egg

demerara sugar

bread

1 Soak the raisins in the Grand Marnier for 10 minutes.

2 Cut the bread into shapes with a cutter. Place the shapes in a bowl with the eggs and cinnamon to soak.

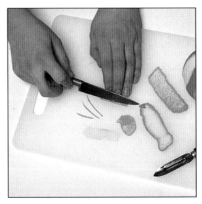

3 Peel the oranges. Remove any excess pith from the peel, then cut it into fine strips and blanch. Refresh it in cold water, then drain.

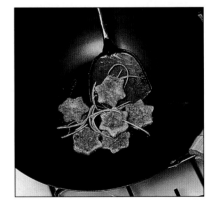

4 Strain the raisins. Heat the wok, then add the oil. When the oil is hot, stir in the butter until melted, then add the bread and fry, turning once, until golden brown. Stir in the raisins and orange rind, and sprinkle with sugar. Serve warm with thick Greek yogurt.

Kentucky Fried Peaches

Never mind your diet, when peaches are this good, it's time for a break!

Serves 4

INGREDIENTS
5 large ripe peaches
50 g/2 oz/4 tbsp butter
30 ml/2 tbsp soft brown sugar
45 ml/3 tbsp Kentucky bourbon
1.2 litres/2 pints/5 cups vanilla
 ice cream
50 g/2 oz/½ cup pecan nuts, toasted

PREPARATION TIME

5 minutes

COOKING TIME

10 minutes

vanilla ice cream

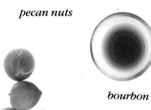
pecan nuts

bourbon

peaches

butter

brown sugar

COOK'S TIP
Peaches that ripen after they are picked will not release their skins when blanched in boiling water.

1 Place the peaches in a large bowl and cover with boiling water to loosen their skins. Drain, refresh under cold running water and slice.

2 Heat the butter in a large frying pan until it foams and begins to brown. Add the sugar, peaches and bourbon, turn up the heat and cook until soft and syrupy. Spoon the hot peaches over the ice cream and decorate with pecan nuts.

INDEX